Small Quilting Projects

Linda Seward

Sterling Publishing Co., Inc.   New York

Edited by Carol Palmer

Library of Congress Cataloging-in-Publication Data

Seward, Linda.
　　Small quilting projects.

　　Includes index.
　　　1. Patchwork—Patterns.　　2. Quilting—Patterns.
I. Title.
TT835.S462　　　1987　　　746.46　　　87-15907
ISBN 0-8069-6740-4
ISBN 0-8069-6692-0 (pbk.)

3　　5　　7　　9　　10　　8　　6　　4　　2

Copyright ©1988 by Linda Seward
Published by Sterling Publishing Co., Inc.
Two Park Avenue, New York, N.Y. 10016
Distributed in Canada by Oak Tree Press Ltd.
% Canadian Manda Group, P.O. Box 920, Station U
Toronto, Ontario, Canada M8Z 5P9
Distributed in the United Kingdom by Blandford Press
Link House, West Street, Poole, Dorset BH15 1LL, England
Distributed in Australia by Capricorn Ltd.
P.O. Box 665, Lane Cove, NSW 2066
Manufactured in the United States of America

For my mother, Evelyn Macho

Acknowledgments

Although a book is usually written by one person, there are often many people behind the scenes, without whom the work wouldn't have been finished to such a high standard. To those people I'd like to express a big thank-you:

Martin Schamus—a belated thanks for introducing my work to Sterling Publishing in the first place. Marty has been a constant source of encouragement and support.

Sharon Falberg, who designed and made the lovely Evening Bag on page 113.

Lisa Benjamin, who gave me the idea for the Sewing Caddy on page 64.

Carol Palmer, my editor, who put up with very cranky letters from an author who feels that not one word should be changed.

Robert, my husband, who is always there when the pieces don't fit, but especially when they do.

Contents

Small Quilting Projects *60-124*

Introduction

When I began working on this book, I wondered if I could think of enough interesting small projects to make in patchwork. I needn't have worried. As I began working, more and more ideas came to me until I realized I had to stop or the book would never be finished! I was surprised at how enthusiastic I became about the projects—after all, they weren't "proper" quilts. But it's amazing how satisfactory it is to complete an item in just a day or so. Small projects are a delight because they are finished almost as soon as they're begun.

My family and friends were astounded at the speed with which these projects were produced. My husband would leave for his office in the morning as I sat in front of my fabric chest with bits and pieces of material spread all around me, only to return in the evening to find a fully finished creation! While I've always been a fast quilter, I couldn't believe how quickly the pieces turned into usable items. I think the reasons are twofold:

1. The projects are small, so fewer pieces are needed to construct them, thus less sewing and quilting are required—all resulting in an enormous saving of time.

2. Because the items are not monumental, you retain the excitement that you always feel at the beginning of a project. There is no possibility of boredom with work that takes so little time to complete. Also, the fabrics remain fresh: when you haven't been looking at them for weeks or months, it's easy to try new and unexpected combinations to see what they'll look like. Because the level of interest is maintained, you can't wait to finish, so that you forget about eating your lunch (a painless way to diet!) or making dinner until the piece is done. (The one necessity is having an understanding family who don't mind leftovers or defrosted soup for dinner again!)

Once, the idea of patchwork brought images of countless hours of cutting, piecing, assembling, and quilting to mind. *Small Quilting Projects* will banish those thoughts forever. You'll have the satisfaction of completing what you started—and in a very short space of time. Because small projects don't require much yardage, you'll be able to dispose of your bags of scraps that have been crying out to be used. And because the items take so little time to complete, this book will be an excellent source of inspiration for quick-to-make gifts for unexpected occasions.

If you don't have enough time to make a large quilt, but you still love patchwork, then this book is for you.

How to Use This Book

This book is arranged for easy use, beginning with *Making Patchwork Projects: Techniques*, which gives instructions on how to piece the patchwork and to quilt. I refer to these vital techniques throughout the book. By familiarizing yourself very thoroughly with this chapter, it will be easy for you to look back and find the technique under discussion. For example, whenever you are required to add a binding, I will refer you to *Binding a Project*; look up the page number in the Index, if necessary. For quilting techniques, you'll be advised to see *How to Quilt*; for intricate sewing, I'll suggest you read *How to Inset* or *Sewing Curves*.

Two more chapters follow the instructions. *Block Designs: 6-Inches Square* consists of 40 distinctive designs for small patchwork blocks which are rated easy, moderate, or challenging. All the blocks are 6-inches square, which means that any block can be used interchangeably with the others. Some designs are traditional; these are presented with a selection of new designs, published here for the first time. From these designs you can create many different projects which are featured in the final chapter, *Small Quilting Projects*.

Small Quilting Projects is divided into four sections: *Sewing Aids*, *For the Kitchen*, *For the Home*, and *Gifts*. You'll find dozens of appealing items to make for yourself, or for your family and friends. Some of these designs are based on the 6-inch square, while others are self-contained. Whichever project you choose, however, you'll find complete instructions along with assembly diagrams and full-size templates, enabling you to make the project with ease. Color photographs of most projects will show you how I interpreted the designs and will provide you with inspiration on possible fabric choices.

METRIC EQUIVALENCY CHART

MM—MILLIMETRES   CM—CENTIMETRES

INCHES TO MILLIMETRES AND CENTIMETRES

INCHES	MM	CM	INCHES	CM	INCHES	CM
⅛	3	0.3	9	22.9	30	76.2
¼	6	0.6	10	25.4	31	78.7
⅜	10	1.0	11	27.9	32	81.3
½	13	1.3	12	30.5	33	83.8
⅝	16	1.6	13	33.0	34	86.4
¾	19	1.9	14	35.6	35	88.9
⅞	22	2.2	15	38.1	36	91.4
1	25	2.5	16	40.6	37	94.0
1¼	32	3.2	17	43.2	38	96.5
1½	38	3.8	18	45.7	39	99.1
1¾	44	4.4	19	48.3	40	101.6
2	51	5.1	20	50.8	41	104.1
2½	64	6.4	21	53.3	42	106.7
3	76	7.6	22	55.9	43	109.2
3½	89	8.9	23	58.4	44	111.8
4	102	10.2	24	61.0	45	114.3
4½	114	11.4	25	63.5	46	116.8
5	127	12.7	26	66.0	47	119.4
6	152	15.2	27	68.6	48	121.9
7	178	17.8	28	71.1	49	124.5
8	203	20.3	29	73.7	50	127.0

YARDS TO METRES

YARDS	METRES	YARDS	METRES	YARDS	METRES	YARDS	METRES	YARDS	METRES
⅛	0.11	2⅛	1.94	4⅛	3.77	6⅛	5.60	8⅛	7.43
¼	0.23	2¼	2.06	4¼	3.89	6¼	5.72	8¼	7.54
⅜	0.34	2⅜	2.17	4⅜	4.00	6⅜	5.83	8⅜	7.66
½	0.46	2½	2.29	4½	4.11	6½	5.94	8½	7.77
⅝	0.57	2⅝	2.40	4⅝	4.23	6⅝	6.06	8⅝	7.89
¾	0.69	2¾	2.51	4¾	4.34	6¾	6.17	8¾	8.00
⅞	0.80	2⅞	2.63	4⅞	4.46	6⅞	6.29	8⅞	8.12
1	0.91	3	2.74	5	4.57	7	6.40	9	8.23
1⅛	1.03	3⅛	2.86	5⅛	4.69	7⅛	6.52	9⅛	8.34
1¼	1.14	3¼	2.97	5¼	4.80	7¼	6.63	9¼	8.46
1⅜	1.26	3⅜	3.09	5⅜	4.91	7⅜	6.74	9⅜	8.57
1½	1.37	3½	3.20	5½	5.03	7½	6.86	9½	8.69
1⅝	1.49	3⅝	3.31	5⅝	5.14	7⅝	6.97	9⅝	8.80
1¾	1.60	3¾	3.43	5¾	5.26	7¾	7.09	9¾	8.92
1⅞	1.71	3⅞	3.54	5⅞	5.37	7⅞	7.20	9⅞	9.03
2	1.83	4	3.66	6	5.49	8	7.32	10	9.14

Making Patchwork Projects: Techniques

Selecting Fabrics & Threads

Each design is accompanied by a screened illustration, an assembly diagram, and a list of templates that tells you how many pieces are needed and their suggested color or value (degree of light or dark): white, light, bright, medium, dark. Bright fabrics can be any color or shade; they are meant to add a flash of unusual or startling color to add spice to the designs. Sometimes, I suggest the word "sky" or "striped" to indicate a color; it is up to you to select a suitable fabric. Follow the block lists, diagrams, and illustrations exactly, or experiment with the placement of colors to create your own interpretation of each design.

Fabrics woven from 100-percent cotton threads are best for quiltmaking, although fabrics with some polyester content can be used. Don't use anything with less than 70-percent cotton, however. Select fabrics with highly contrasting values. Unorthodox combinations are fine and fun to use—especially in a small project. Select an attractive interplay of solid fabrics (or fabrics with a tiny all-over print), fabrics with a medium-scale print and at least one with a large-scale print.

Because of the small size of the projects in this book, it won't always be necessary to purchase new fabric. In many cases, only a few scraps are needed to complete an entire project. Check your rag bag before buying new fabrics. You may find that this book will enable you to finally use up all those old materials that have been haunting you, thus giving you lots of room (and an excuse) to buy new fabrics!

If you are buying new fabrics, try to buy all fabrics for your project at the same time. You can best see how colors and patterns work with one another while they are still on the bolt. Matching fabrics from small scraps is very difficult and quite often doesn't work when you take the new selections home.

If in doubt about yardages, always buy *more* fabric than you think you'll need. Dye lots vary considerably; often, by the time you realize that you'll need more fabric, it may be too late to find the same dye lot. The fabric yardages listed for each project are exact and assume your cutting is precise. If you're not sure about the accuracy of your cutting, buy a little more fabric—you can always use the leftover pieces in some future creation.

When you are satisfied with your fabric choices, buy your sewing thread—an unobtrusive color that will blend with all the fabrics.

Washing & Straightening

Prewash all fabrics to be used in your project. Wash fabrics of a similar color in the very hottest water and hang them to dry (tangling in a clothes dryer can twist the fabrics off-grain). To wash scraps, place similar colors in a net bag before putting in the machine—this will eliminate much of the inevitable fraying that occurs. Before putting new fabrics in the washing machine, clip into the selvages (finished edges) at 2-inch intervals to accommodate shrinkage. If there is any evidence that the fabric is not colorfast (the colors will bleed), wash the fabric again; or soak it in a solution of 3 parts cold water and 1 part white vinegar. Rinse the fabric and spread it on a white towel while wet. If there is still evidence of color bleeding, discard the fabric and select another. It is better to make this effort in the beginning than to experience the horror of washing a finished project only to find that it has been ruined by bleeding fabrics. If possible, iron the fabrics while they are slightly damp; the dampness makes it easier to remove all the wrinkles. Trim away any frayed edges.

Check the grain. The crosswise and lengthwise threads of the fabric should be exactly perpendicular to each other. If they aren't perpendicular grasp the four corners of the fabric and pull diagonally from opposite corners simultaneously to straighten the grain (this is better done with two pairs of hands). Repeat this pulling alternately from opposite corners until the threads are perpendicular to one another.

Prepare the fabrics for cutting as follows: Accurately cut off any selvages or uneven edges. To do this, measure an even distance from each edge (selvages are usually ¼ inch but can be as wide as ½ inch); draw a cutting line with a pencil and ruler. Cut away the edges along the pencil line. Next, using a triangle and a ruler, draw a line across the fabric that is exactly perpendicular to the cut edge (Fig. 1). Cut away any excess fabric beyond this line. You are now ready to make your templates, mark your fabric and cut out your pieces.

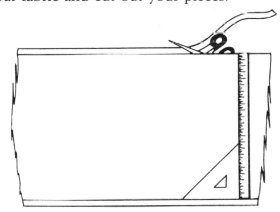

Fig. 1   Cutting away the selvages

Making Templates & Cutting the Pieces

Using tracing paper and a pencil, trace the templates for the designs you have chosen. Mark each tracing with the name of the design, the letter of the template (the letter "I" is not used for templates in this book) and the value(s) of the fabric(s) from which it should be cut.

Glue the tracing to medium-weight cardboard or plastic; allow the glue to dry. Cut out each template using an X-acto knife or other cutting blade. For straight lines, use a straight metal edge to guide the knife.

The edge of the template is the sewing line; therefore, a ¼-inch seam allowance *must be added* when marking the templates on the fabric. The best way to do this is by drawing a ¼-inch seam allowance on the wrong side of the fabric along the lengthwise and crosswise cut edges (Fig. 2). You can then place the edge of your template on the marked line. Trace around the edge of your template. Use a ruler to mark a ¼-inch seam allowance around each of the remaining edges before marking the next template. Continue to mark all your templates on the wrong side of the fabric in this way.

To avoid waste and conserve fabric, mark your pieces so that they can be cut along a mutual edge (Fig. 3 and Fig. 4). As a rule, the longest edge of any template should be placed on the straight (lengthwise) grain of the fabric. *All* edges of squares and rectangles should be on the straight grain.

Follow the list given with each design for the number of pieces to be cut and how to cut them. Symmetrical pieces do not need to be flipped over or "reversed," but many of the designs are made up of asymmetrical pieces, thus their mirror image or reverse side is needed to complete a pattern. This need to reverse is always indicated with each list. When a design is asymmetrical and you are not instructed to reverse the template, it means the template has already been reversed for you. Where the list indicates a number of pieces are "reversed," turn your template over to the opposite (wrong) side and mark the necessary number of pieces on the fabric. You can check your work by studying the assembly diagram of your block.

After you have marked your pieces, carefully cut them out along the cutting lines. *Accuracy*—in both marking and cutting—is essential to the successful completion of each project. If you are cutting out all of your pieces at once, carefully gather and keep the pieces for each project in a separate envelope or plastic bag to avoid confusion when sewing time arrives.

Fig. 2

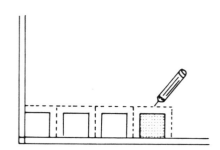

Fig. 3

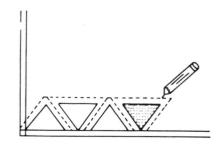

Fig. 4

Rotary Cutting

While writing this book I was introduced to the rotary cutter, which forever changed my outlook on cutting out patchwork pieces for certain projects. Using a rotary cutter for simple shapes—strips, squares, rectangles, and triangles—will halve the amount of time you spend on a project.

The Picnic Set on pages 120–124 was the first project I made with a rotary cutter, and though the blanket is not technically "small," I included it in this book because it took me less time to make than most of the other projects half its size! The secret lies in cutting several layers at the same time.

Only 3 pieces of equipment are required for rotary cutting, and while the initial expense may be more than you might wish to spend, the saving in time and the unbelievable accuracy you'll achieve will more than make up for what you pay. You'll need a rotary cutter with a *large* wheel, a cutting board specially designed for a rotary cutter, and a thick plastic ruler with marked grid or cutting lines. These items can be found in any well-stocked quilting shop. The cutting board can also be found in most art supply shops; ask for the "self-healing" type.

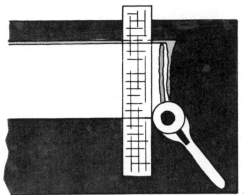

Fig. 5

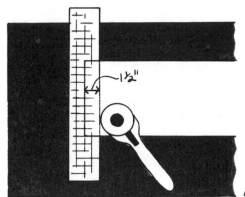

Fig. 6

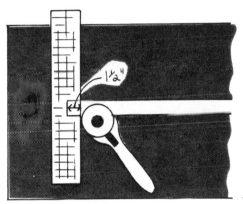

Fig. 7

About 4–6 layers of material can be cut at one time, depending upon the fabric weight. Beginners should work with 4 layers. To prepare the fabric, fold in half on the straight grain with selvages matching, and steam-press. Fold in half again, creating 4 layers, and press again. Without unfolding it, place the fabric on the cutting board, then place your ruler on the fabric, aligning one of the grid lines with the pressed folded edge. Holding the ruler firmly on the fabric, run the blade of the rotary cutter along the edge of the ruler; this will cut away any ragged edges and straighten your fabric on the grain (Fig. 5). Always push the blade *away* from you when cutting fabrics.

You are now ready to cut strips. Decide upon the width of the strips you require, then add ½ inch for seam allowances. For example, if your project requires 1-inch strips, your strip will need to be 1½ inches to accommodate the ¼-inch seam allowances at each edge. (For ease in cutting for right-handed quilters, move the fabric so your straight outer edge is at the left of the cutting board; left-handed quilters should reverse these instructions.) Position the ruler on the fabric so your cutting edge is 1½ inches away from the outer edge of the fabric (Fig. 6). Run the blade of your rotary cutter along the edge of the ruler to cut the strip. To cut squares, trim one edge of the strip to remove the folds. Turn the strip and measure 1½ inches away from the cut end; cut along this measurement and you'll have 4 perfect squares (Fig. 7). If you measure correctly and cut firmly, your squares will be extremely accurate without having to use a template!

Strips, such as those used for the Picnic Set or for Seminole Patchwork (pages 60–61) are cut in seconds using a rotary cutter. Save any leftover strips in a bag for a future scrap project. Try this technique and you'll never cut strips or other simple shapes with scissors again!

13

Sewing the Pieces: Patchwork

I assume you will use a sewing machine to sew the pieces or patches for each project, although it is perfectly acceptable (though much slower) to do the piecing by hand.

Each design is accompanied by complete piecing instructions. Most designs are assembled in subunits (squares, triangles, strips) that are then joined to complete the design.

When sewing pieces together, match the raw edges carefully, pinning them together at each end

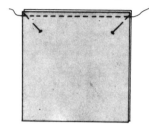

Fig. 8

if necessary (Fig. 8). Sew the pieces together in chains to save time (Fig. 9). Always press the seams to one side, preferably towards the darker fabric (Fig. 10).

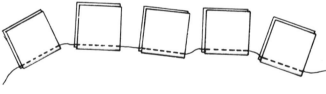

Fig. 9

When sewing sub-units together, carefully match the seams before you sew, pinning the pieces at crucial points (Fig. 11). When matching seams, it is best to press seam allowances in opposite directions.

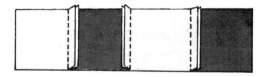

Fig. 10

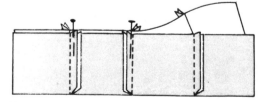

Fig. 11

HOW TO INSET

Sometimes, pieces of a design must be inset into one another. While this procedure is slightly tricky at first, it is possible to get perfect corners every time by using the following method:

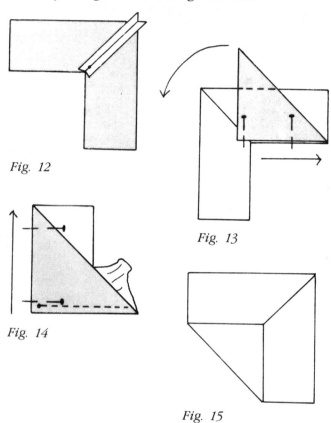

Fig. 12

Fig. 14

Fig. 13

Fig. 15

1. A triangular or square piece is inset into two other pieces that are sewn together to form an angle (Fig. 12). When sewing the pieces that form the angle together, end your stitching ¼-inch away from the edge to be inset (shown by the dot in the diagram).

2. Pin the piece to be inset along one edge of the angle (Fig. 13) and stitch from the middle (dot) to the edge (in the direction of the arrow).

3. Folding the excess fabric out of the way, pin the unsewn edges together and stitch from the central point to the outer edge (Fig. 14).

4. Open out the fabrics and carefully steam-press (Fig. 15). If you notice any puckers at the corner, you can usually eliminate them by removing a stitch from one of the seams just sewn.

SEWING CURVES

Curved edges are time-consuming to sew, but quite rewarding when finished. Excellent results can be achieved by following this procedure:

1. Clip the curve of the concave piece (Fig. 16).

2. Pin the clipped piece to the convex piece, matching the right angles at the corners first, then easing the curved edge to fit; stitch (Fig. 17).

3. Open out the fabrics and steam-press carefully (Fig. 18).

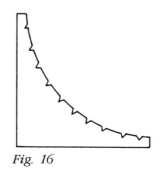

Fig. 16

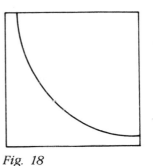

Fig. 17

HOW TO APPLIQUÉ

"Appliqué" means to apply to a larger surface, or in this technique, to apply one piece of fabric over another. While this book mainly features patchwork (or pieced) designs, there are some examples that require small decorative touches to be appliquéd in place. Hand appliqué is recommended.

Press the seam allowance ¼ inch to the wrong side and baste in place, if desired.

Place the pressed appliqué in its correct position on your patchwork. Slip-stitch in place using tiny invisible stitches. Backstitch at the end to secure your thread.

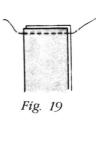

Fig. 18

Special Techniques

Your can use special techniques to enhance or finish a project; these are referred to throughout the book.

RUFFLE

Cut the fabric strip to the required size, piecing the strip, if necessary, for additional length. With right sides together, stitch the short ends to each other (Fig. 19), forming a continuous circle of fabric. Fold the fabric in half lengthwise with wrong sides together and press; machine-baste ¼ inch away from the raw edges all around (Fig. 20). Gently pull the basting stitches, gathering the ruffle to approximately fit the edges of the project (Fig. 21). With raw edges even, pin the ruffle to the right side of the project, adjusting the gathers evenly to fit; allow extra gathers or make a pleat at each of the corners (Fig. 22). Stitch the ruffle securely to the project.

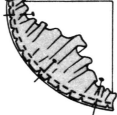

Fig. 19

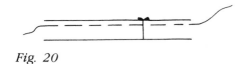

Fig. 20

Fig. 21

LACE

With raw edges even, pin the lace to the right side of the project; allow extra gathers or make a pleat at each of the corners (Fig. 22). Overlap the beginning and end of the lace by about ¼ inch; then stitch the lace securely to the project.

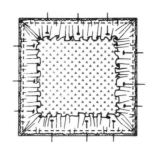

Fig. 22

PIPING

Cut the fabric strip to the required size, piecing the strip, if necessary, for additional length. Place the piping cord on the middle of the wrong side of the fabric; then fold the fabric in half lengthwise, enclosing the piping cord. Using a zipper foot on the sewing machine, stitch close to the cord (Fig. 23). Trim the seam allowance to ¼ inch. Pin the piping to the right side of the project with raw edges even. To ease the piping around each corner, clip into the seam allowance to the stitching line (Fig. 24). Continue pinning the piping in place until you reach the beginning. Overlap the beginning of the piping by 1 inch; then cut away any excess. Remove 1 inch of stitching from the end of the piping, push back the excess fabric and trim away only the cord so that the beginning and end of the cord are flush (Fig. 25). Now straighten out the excess fabric and fingerpress the raw edge ½ inch to the wrong side (inside) by running your finger over the fold a few times. Slip the beginning of the piping inside the end so that the excess fabric covers all raw edges (Fig. 26); pin in place. Stitch the piping to the project all around.

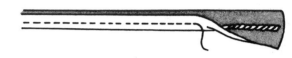

Fig. 23

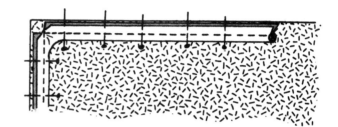

Fig. 24

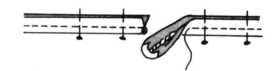

Fig. 25

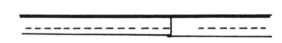

Fig. 26

EMBROIDERY

Hand embroidery can add a very special touch to a patchwork project. Often a few simple lines of embroidery can make a design come to life. Use any standard 6-strand cotton embroidery floss (thread).

If embroidery lines are given on a design, transfer the lines to the right side of your fabric using a hard lead pencil and graphite paper; or you can draw the design freehand on the fabric with a pencil.

Stretch the area to be embroidered in an embroidery hoop to hold the fabric taut; reposition the hoop as necessary while you are working. If the fabric sags in the hoop, pull it taut again. Embroider the design following the individual directions and stitch details (Fig. 27).

Outline stitch

Satin stitch   **Straight stitch**

Fig. 27 Embroidery stitch details

Each time you begin embroidering, leave extra thread dangling on the back of the fabric and embroider over it as you work to secure, holding the thread flat against the fabric with your free hand. Do not make knots. To end a strand or begin a new one, weave the floss under the stitches on the back. From time to time, allow the needle and floss to hang straight down to unwind; this will prevent the floss from kinking or twisting while you embroider.

HOW TO MITRE CORNERS

Fold the raw ends of adjacent border or binding strips back on themselves to form a 45° angle (Fig. 28). Press. Pin and sew the edges together, matching the creases formed by the pressing. Check the right side to make sure that the corner is perfect, with no puckers. If there are puckers, you can usually correct them by removing one of the stitches. If the corner is perfect (Fig. 29), trim away the excess seam allowance, leaving a ¼-inch seam allowance. Press carefully.

LOOPS & TIES

Many of the projects in this book are meant to be hung or attached to something in some way. Loops and ties are made quickly and easily in a fabric that matches the binding.

Cut your chosen fabric to the size indicated for your project. Press the strip in half lengthwise, wrong sides together. Open the strip and press each of the long raw edges exactly to the pressed central fold, again with the wrong sides together. Fold and press each of the short ends ¼ inch to the wrong side; then press the strip in half again, sandwiching all raw edges inside; topstitch the folded edges together. Attach the loops or ties to the project following the individual instructions.

USING A TUBE TURNER

A tube turner can be used to turn a loop, tie or strap inside out. There are 2 types of tube turners. The standard American style has a hook with a catch at the end as illustrated in Figs. 30 and 31; the British version has an eye at the end.

Stitch a strip of fabric together lengthwise with wrong sides facing, forming a tube. Insert the tube turner into the tube, gathering the strip onto the tube turner as necessary. Hook the end of the tube

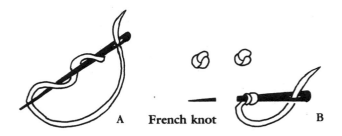

A   French knot   B

Fig. 27   Embroidery stitch details continued

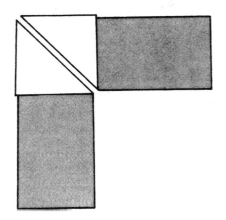

Fig. 28

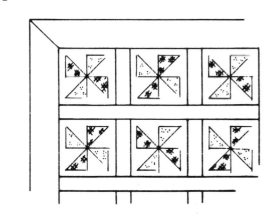

Fig. 29

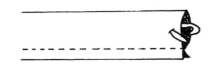

Fig. 30

Fig. 31

turner through the edge of the fabric, and work the catch so it holds the fabric securely in the hook (Fig. 30); or sew the eye of the tube turner to the edge of the fabric using the thread ends of the seam allowances. Ease the fabric back over the tube turner, working it along section by section. Pull until the strip turns right-side out (Fig. 31).

MAKING A BUTTONHOLE

Buttonholes made on the sewing machine are very quick and easy to do. First, lightly mark the position of the buttonhole on the fabric using a pencil. Attach a buttonhole foot to your sewing machine and set the machine as instructed in your manual. Work the buttonhole as directed in the manual. The usual method is to work a line of close zigzag satin stitches the entire length of the buttonhole (Fig. 32a). Zigzag back and forth at the bottom to secure the end, then satin-stitch back to the beginning; work more zigzag stitches at the beginning to secure that end (Fig. 32b). Finally, work a

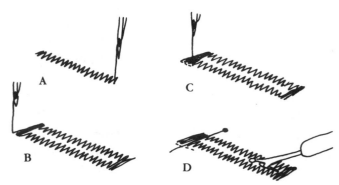

Fig. 32

few stitches along the side of the buttonhole to secure the threads (Fig. 32c). Remove the fabric from the sewing machine. Using a seam ripper or a small pair of sharp scissors, carefully slit the buttonhole, placing a pin at the end of the buttonhole to prevent yourself from cutting too far (Fig. 32d).

If you do not have a sewing machine, or if you have a machine that does not do buttonholes, you can substitue Velcro, snap fasteners or a hook and eye.

Batting

Batting, the central core of a quilted project, is available in polyester, cotton, and wool. For washability and ease in handling, select a polyester batting; it can be purchased in many sizes and weights. It is best to use a thin batting for small projects to keep the puffiness in scale with the size of the finished design. A thicker batting can be used for larger projects, such as blankets and wall hangings or for designs that are quilted and then stuffed, such as pillows.

Cotton and wool battings are a bit more difficult to handle, but quilters who prefer pure natural fibres strongly recommend them. Projects made with cotton or wool battings must be quilted at 1½-inch intervals to prevent lumps from forming when the project is washed. It is best to dry-clean projects made with cotton or wool batting, however.

Assembling a Project for Quilting

A quilt is actually like a sandwich, with the batting as the filling and the top and back as the bread. To make the sandwich, you'll need a large flat surface, such as a worktable or the floor.

Iron the back very well; tape it to the work surface, wrong side up, with the grain straight and all corners making 90° angles. Carefully place the batting over the middle of the back. If you must piece the batting, butt the edges and baste them together with large cross stitches.

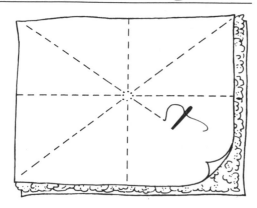

Fig. 33

Press the pieced top carefully—this will be the last time it will be ironed, so make the pressing a good one. Trim away any uneven seams on the back, and any threads or ravelled edges. When you are satisfied, set the top, right side up, over the batting to match the outside edges.

Baste the three layers together quite thoroughly: First baste diagonally from the middle to each cor-ner, then crosswise and lengthwise (Fig. 30). If you are using a quilting frame, put the quilt into the frame. If quilting with a hoop, add some additional basting (concentric squares) for extra safety.

You are now ready to quilt.

How to Quilt

You'll need a quilting or "between" needle, size 7 through 10 (10 is smallest); an 8 needle is a good size for most quilters. A thimble for the middle finger of your sewing hand is essential as is strong, mercerized 100-percent cotton quilting thread. Some quilters like to use a second thimble on the index finger of the hand under the quilt; this is optional.

To begin, cut an 18-inch length of quilting thread; thread your needle and knot the end of the thread. Run the needle and thread through the pieced top and some of the batting, pulling the knot beneath the surface of the quilt top (it usual-ly makes a satisfying "popping" sound) and bury-ing it in the batting (Fig. 34).

The quilting stitch is basically a running stitch. Hold the index finger of your left hand (for right-handed quilters) or right hand (for left-handed quilters) beneath the project just below the spot where you wish to make your stitches. Try to achieve a smooth rhythm, rocking your needle from the surface to the back, and then returning it again to the surface. Try to make 3 to 4 stitches at a time. Fig. 35 shows how to use the thimble to help push the needle through the fabric; the il-lustration also shows how the finger beneath pushes against the project to compress the batting, making it easier to take several stitches at a time. Fig. 36 is a cross-section diagram showing how the quilting stitches should look when done correctly.

Don't panic if your stitches look larger than you think they should—an *even line* of stitches is the important thing, not the size of the stitches. The more you quilt, the smaller your stitches will become, but in the beginning, concentrate on making the stitches the same length on the top and on the back.

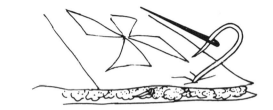

Fig. 34

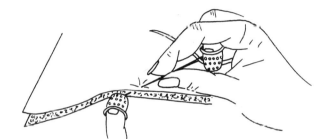

Fig. 35

Fig. 36

Suggestions for how to quilt each project are given at the end of each set of piecing instructions. For more quilting ideas, see Fig. 37 and also the finished projects shown on the color pages.

If you are using a hoop, baste strips of fabric, 6 to 12 inches wide, to the edges of the project so that it can be held in the hoop when you are quilting the outer edges.

In addition to the traditional type of quilting just described, three other methods are often used to quilt: machine quilting, the tufting stitch, and the quilt-as-you-go method. Follow the instructions below for each method.

19

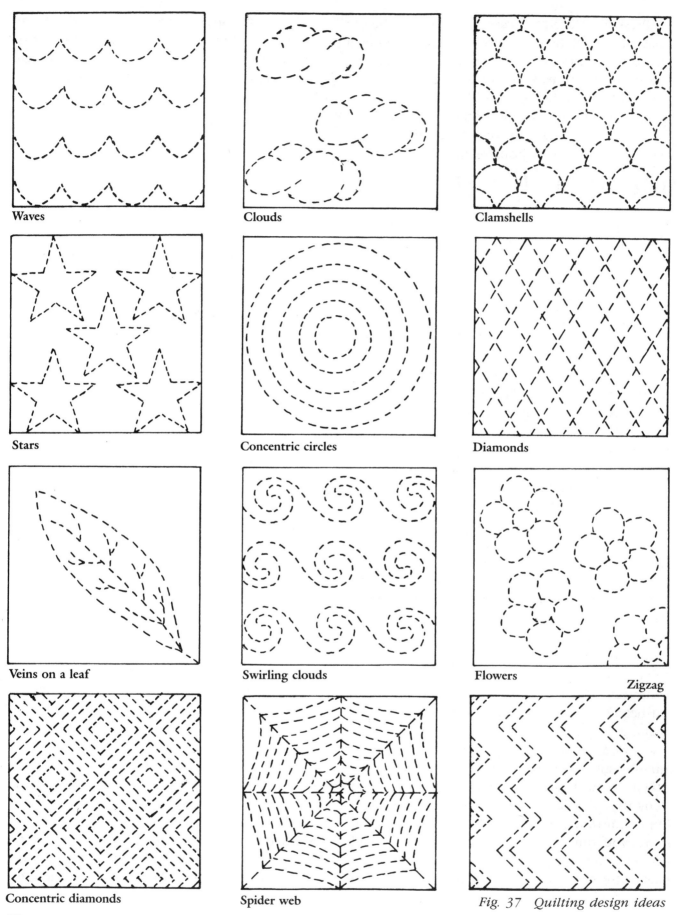

Waves

Clouds

Clamshells

Stars

Concentric circles

Diamonds

Veins on a leaf

Swirling clouds

Flowers

Zigzag

Concentric diamonds

Spider web

Fig. 37 Quilting design ideas

20

MACHINE QUILTING

Insert a size-14 needle in your machine, loosen the thread tension slightly, and set the stitch length for 12 stitches per inch. Use a zig-zag foot or attach a quilting foot if you have one. Spread the layers of your well-basted project under the machine foot with your hands to imitate the tension of a quilting frame. Stitch slowly. Always machine-quilt in the same direction across a project to prevent the layers from shifting. To prevent the top layer from easing ahead of the needle when sewing a long line, pin the 3 layers together directly over each line to be quilted.

Each time you begin and end a line of stitching, the thread ends must be finished-off, which can be very time-consuming. For speedier machine quilting, adapt your designs so as to quilt in a continuous line, thus avoiding finishing-off the threads too many times. To end a line of machine quilting, turn the project to the wrong side, and pull the thread end gently, drawing up the thread from the right side. Pull through gently. Knot the threads. Insert both threads into a needle and run them through the back and batting, bringing the needle out at least one inch away. Pull gently and clip away excess thread close to fabric so that the ends will pop back into the batting out of sight.

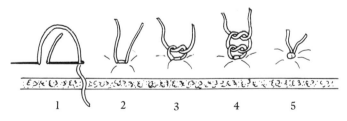

Fig. 38

TUFTING STITCH

The tufting stitch can be used on the right or wrong side of a project, depending upon whether or not you wish the knot to show. Following Fig. 38 and using a length of quilting thread, make a backstitch through all 3 layers of the project (1); the ends should be even (2). Tie the ends in a simple knot (3); tie another knot over the first (4). Pull tight and trim the ends close to the knot (5).

QUILT-AS-YOU-GO METHOD

Use the quilt-as-you-go technique for simple patchwork designs; piecing and quilting are done at the same time using a sewing machine. This method considerably shortens the time needed to make a project because when the sewing is done, the project is finished (except for the binding).

Follow the requirements for the project you are making to cut the back and batting pieces; the batting should be ¼-inch smaller than the back at each edge. Place the batting on the middle of the wrong side of the back; baste in place diagonally or horizontally and vertically so that the threads will cross in the exact middle of the block; these lines will serve as guidelines for placement of the patchwork. Place the basted piece, batting side up, on a flat surface. Position the first patchwork piece, right side up, on the batting and baste in place all

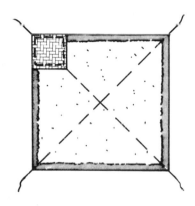

Fig. 39

around (Fig. 39). Pin the second piece over the first with right sides together and raw edges even. Stitch together ¼ inch from the edge, making sure all the layers feed smoothly under the presser foot of the sewing machine (Fig. 40). Remove the pins and fold

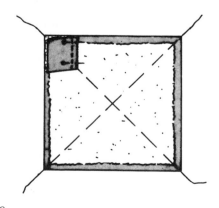

Fig. 40

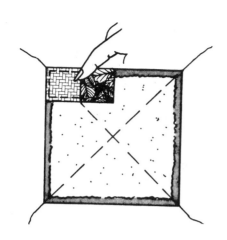

Fig. 41

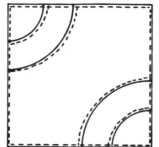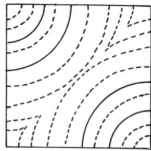

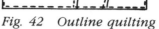

Fig. 42 Outline quilting   Fig. 43 Echo quilting

the second piece to the right side; finger-press by running your finger over the seam a few times (Fig. 41). (Do not be tempted to use an iron for pressing or you may be faced with melted batting!) Continue adding pieces, as directed, until the entire base is covered, finger-pressing after each new piece is added. Complete the project, following the individual instructions.

OUTLINE QUILTING

Work one row of quilting around the edge of a piece, either in the seam (called quilting "in-the-ditch") or just next to the seam as shown in the illustration (Fig. 42).

ECHO QUILTING

Work parallel lines of quilting to emphasize a portion of a design (Fig. 43). Lines can be ¼ to ½ inch apart, depending upon the size of the project. This is called "echo quilting" because the lines of stitching parallel or "echo" the shape of the piece you wish to accentuate.

Binding a Project

When the quilting is finished, remove your basting stitches. You are now ready for the final step—the binding. The binding is the finishing touch to your project and should be used to enhance the overall design; give it careful consideration. All project requirements include the measurements for a separate binding, although many of the projects can be finished with self-binding or fold-finishing (see below). Usually, the binding is cut on the straight grain of the fabric, but there are times when the binding must be cut on the bias. While I usually do not recommend using a purchased binding, for a small project with curved edges, such as a pot holder, it would be far easier—and much quicker!—to use double-fold bias tape.

SEPARATE BINDING

A separate binding takes a bit more time to prepare than a self-binding, but it gives you the freedom to choose any preferred color or print.

To prepare a separate binding, cut your chosen fabric to the length indicated with the requirements

for your project. For a larger project, such as a blanket, piecing will be necessary. Press the strip in half lengthwise, wrong sides together. Open the strip and press one long raw edge exactly to the pressed central fold, again with the wrong sides together; this folded edge is later slip-stitched to the back of the project.

With right sides together and raw edges even, pin the unpressed edge of the binding to the right side of the project. If you are binding a project with corners, allow extra fabric at each corner for mitring. For most other projects, about ¼ inch excess fabric should extend beyond each edge of the piece you are binding; this excess fabric is later folded under to conceal the raw edges.

Start your stitching at the edge and stitch to the opposite edge, making a ¼-inch seam. Wrap the pressed edge of the binding over the raw edges of the project to the back; slip-stitch invisibly in place, folding the excess fabric at each end under to conceal the raw edges. Complete each strip of binding in turn before adding the next one.

SELF-BINDING

Self-binding is a quick and easy way to finish a quilted project. This technique is not always recommended when the back is made from the same fabric as the border because of the finished effect: self-binding can make the edges of the project seem to fade away, particularly if the colors of the project are very strong.

If you decide to self-bind your project, mark and cut an extra inch all around the edge of the fabric for the back; this will add 2 inches to the length and width measurements. (Most projects include fabric for a self-binding in the measurements given for the back.) Arrange the batting and top carefully over the lining to leave the inch-wide border free around the edges.

After the quilting is done, you can bind the project. Finger-press the edges of the back ½ inch inward to the wrong side of the fabric to make a folded edge. Then wrap the back towards the pieced top, covering the edges of the batting and top. Pin the folded edge to the top (Fig. 44). Slip-stitch the folded edge of the back invisibly to the top. Mitre the corners or conceal the raw ends, as necessary. Remove all pins when finished.

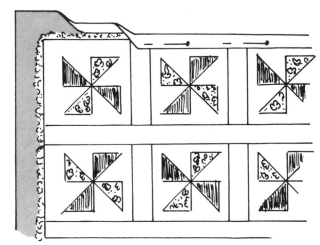

Fig. 44

FOLD-FINISHING

This type of "binding" should be done *before* the project has been quilted. Trim the raw edges of the back even with the top; then fold the raw edges of both the top and back ¼ inch towards each other to conceal the raw edges inside the project. Slip-stitch together invisibly and securely. To quilt, baste strips of muslin to the finished edge of the project so that it can be placed in a frame or hoop.

Hanging a Patchwork Project

When a project is meant to be hung on a wall, measurements are always given for a sleeve. To attach a sleeve to a project, turn all raw edges ¼ inch to the wrong side; repeat the folding and topstitch in place so that all raw edges are hidden. Press. Pin the sleeve flat across the top of the project on the back, centering it between the sides. Slip-stitch each long edge of the sleeve securely to the project back; do not allow your stitches to go through to the right side. Insert a rod through the sleeve for hanging.

If you prefer to hang the project from a strap, cut a length of fabric 1½ inches wide by 3 inches plus the width of the top of the project. For example, the top of the Letter Holder is 10 inches wide, so the strip should be 1½" × 13". Fold the strip in half lengthwise with right sides facing and edges even. Stitch the long edges and one short edge together, making ¼-inch seams. Turn to the right side using a tube turner. Press carefully. Fold the raw edges at the open end ¼ inch inside and slip-stitch closed. Make and attach a sleeve as directed above and insert a ruler or rod inside to keep the top of the project straight. Stitch the ends of the strap securely to the back on each side of the sleeve.

Your Signature

Your project will have greater personal and historic value if it is signed and dated. Embroider your name and the date on the front or back with embroidery floss or sign your name and date on the back with indelible ink.

Block Designs: 6-Inches Square

*T*he 40 designs in this chapter are all 6-inches square, which means that any design can be used interchangeably with the rest. For ease in selection, the blocks have been rated according to the level of expertise needed. Easy designs have straight seams with simple matching—these are excellent patterns for beginners to choose. Moderate designs may have a large number of pieces, angled seams, or pieces that are a bit tricky to match—these are recommended for novice quilters. Challenging designs may have inset seams, curved seams, or pieces that require very careful matching and sewing—a bit of expertise is required.

Choose a theme when making a project. For example, you may wish to use only flower designs for a table runner or letter holder; select from Flower Cross, Spring Blossom, Deco Flower, English Thistle, and Flower Pot. If you are making the Kitchen Set, why not use designs appropriate to a kitchen such as Corn & Beans, Broken Dishes, Broken Sugar Bowl, and Cups & Saucers. For a wedding or anniversary gift, use Crossroads, Happy Marriage, Love in a Mist, Contrary Wife, or Single Wedding Ring.

Use your imagination to make the projects meaningful to you and the recipient. Because the choice of blocks for the projects in the last chapter is entirely up to you, your creation is bound to be completely different from anyone else's. Also, because of the wide range of choices, you needn't ever make the same project twice.

All That Jazz

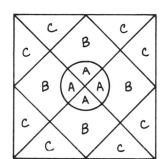

Fig. 45

Challenging
Pieces per block: 16
A *2 light, 2 bright*
B *2 light, 2 bright*
C *8 striped*

Add depth to this design by using a striped fabric around the edges. The curved seams are a bit of a challenge; see *How to Sew Curves*. The block is composed of 4 large triangles. Templates are on page 27.

To begin, sew each light A to a bright B, and each bright A to a light B, easing each A carefully into B. Next sew a C to each long, unpieced edge of B.

Sew 2 pairs of triangles together to make each half of the block, being careful to sew contrasting pieces together as shown in the diagram. Finally, sew the halves together, matching seams carefully, to complete the design.

Quilt along the curved seam of the central circle, then echo-quilt the circle every ½ inch across the entire block.

Crossroads

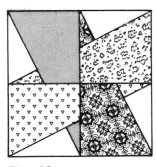

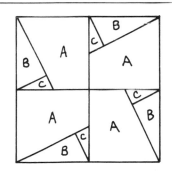

Fig. 46

The "overlapping" triangles give this design a 3-dimensional appearance. It is very easily assembled in 4 squares. Follow the screened assembly diagram carefully when constructing the squares to get the colors in the correct positions.

The templates are on page 27. To make each square, sew B to C, then sew B-C to A; be sure to follow the sequence of colors shown in the diagram. Sew 2 pairs of squares together for each half of the design. Sew the halves together, matching seams carefully, to complete the design.

Outline-quilt every seam.

Easy
Pieces per block: 12
Easy
Pieces per block: 24
A *1 light* I, *1 bright, 1 medium, 1 dark*
B *4 light* II
C *1 light* I, *1 bright, 1 medium, 1 dark*

Bow

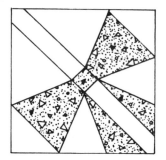

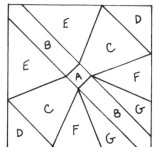

Fig. 47

Moderate
Pieces per block: 13

A	1 medium	E	1 light, 1 light
B	2 light		reversed
C	2 medium	F	2 light
D	2 light	G	1 medium, 1
			medium reversed

Pretty and feminine, this block will enhance any project you make for a female friend or relation. Arrange all the pieces on a flat surface before beginning, to prevent confusion about the placement of the E, F and G pieces.

To begin, sew the B's to opposite sides of A for the central strip. For the side triangles, sew each D to a C. Sew G to F, then sew E and F to opposite sides of C.

Sew the side triangles to each long edge of the central strip, matching seams carefully.

Outline-quilt the bow and its streamers, then quilt parallel lines within these pieces to resemble grosgrain ribbon.

Jazz Bow

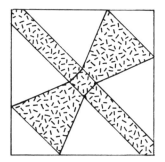

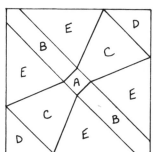

Fig. 48

Easy
Pieces per block: 11

A	1 medium	D	2 light
B	2 medium	E	2 light, 2 light
C	2 medium		reversed

The male counterpart to Bow (above), this design is witty and distinctive. It is composed of a central strip flanked by 2 side triangles.

For the central strip, sew the B's to opposite sides of A. For the side triangles, sew a D to each C, then sew the E's to opposite sides of each C.

Sew the side triangles to each long edge of the central strip, matching seams carefully in the middle.

Outline-quilt the medium pieces.

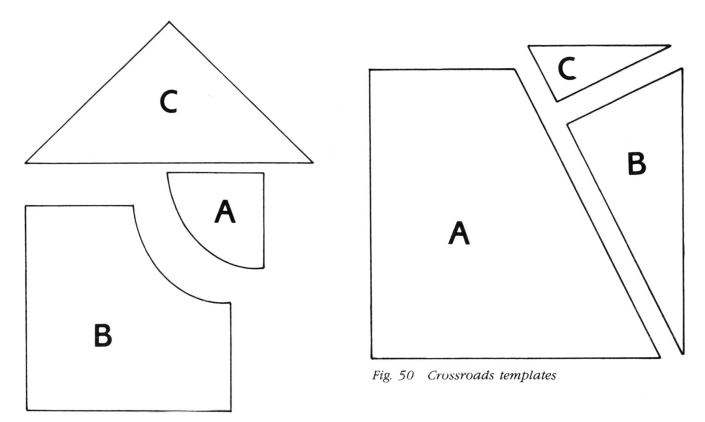

Fig. 49   All That Jazz templates

Fig. 50   Crossroads templates

Fig. 51   Bow and Jazz Bow combined templates

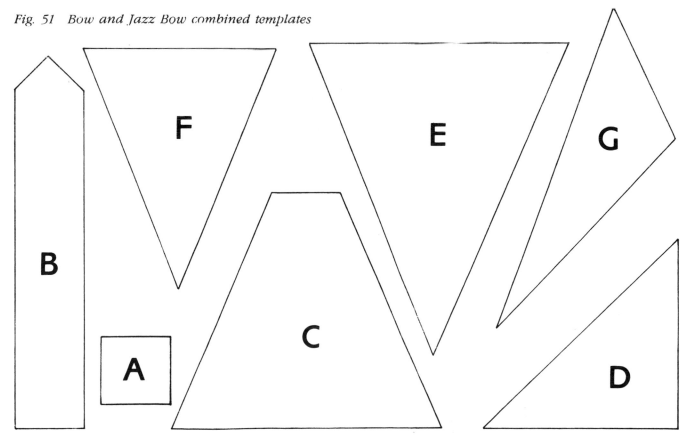

Belt Buckle

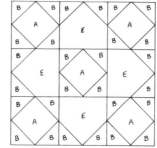

Fig. 52

Easy
Pieces per block: 37
A   2 bright, 3 medium
B   20 light, 8 dark
E   4 dark

Although there are a lot of pieces, this design is all straight and easy sewing. Arrange the pieces first on a flat surface to achieve the correct position of the fabrics.

Construct the 5 A-B squares first by sewing a B to each edge of each A. Next sew a B to each angled edge of each E.

Arrange the squares in 3 rows with 3 squares in each row as shown in the diagram. Sew the squares together in rows, then sew the rows together, matching seams carefully, to complete the design.

Outline-quilt the dark "buckle," then quilt around the bright and medium "belt" pieces.

Flower Cross

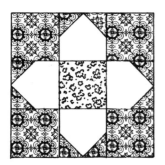

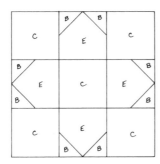

Fig. 53

Easy
Pieces per block: 17
B   8 dark
C   1 medium, 4 dark
E   4 light

Make the flower in a light fabric against a dark background as shown, or for a different look, make a dark flower against a pale background.

To begin, sew a B to each angled edge of E. Arrange the pieced squares alternately with the C squares in 3 rows with 3 squares in each row. Place the medium C in the middle of the block.

Sew the squares together in rows, then sew the rows together, matching seams carefully, to complete the design.

Outline-quilt the flower petals.

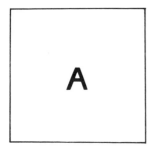

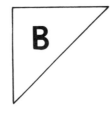

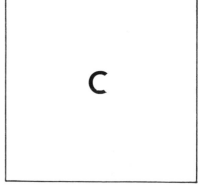

Fig. 54   *Combined templates for Belt Buckle, Flower Cross, Coming of Spring, and Devil's Advocate*

Coming of Spring

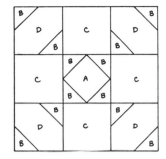

Fig. 55

Easy
Pieces per block: 21
A   1 light
B   4 light, 8 dark
C   4 dark
D   4 bright

Wonderful effects can be achieved by sewing several of these blocks together with edges matching—multiple design possibilities are created.

To begin, sew a dark B to each edge of A. Sew a dark and light B to opposite edges of each D.

Following the diagram, arrange the pieced squares and the C squares in 3 rows with 3 squares in each row. Sew the squares together in rows, then sew the rows together, matching seams carefully, to complete the design.

Outline-quilt the medium and dark pieces.

Devil's Advocate

(Color Illus. 15B)

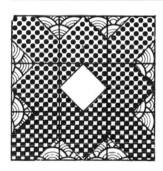
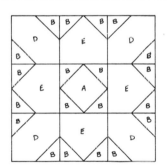

Fig. 56

Easy
Pieces per block: 29
A   1 light
B   4 bright, 16 dark
D   4 bright
E   4 bright

Try this wicked design in a new project—use devilish colors such as red, black and white. It's very quick and easy to make.

To begin, sew the 4 bright B pieces to each edge of A. Next sew a dark B to opposite sides of each D. Finally, sew a dark B to the angled edges of each E.

Arrange the pieces in 3 rows with 3 squares in each row as shown in the diagram. Sew the squares together in rows, then sew the rows together, matching seams carefully, to complete the design.

Outline-quilt the edge of A, then quilt around the outer edges of the bright pieces.

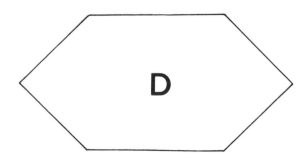

D

Fig. 54   *continued*

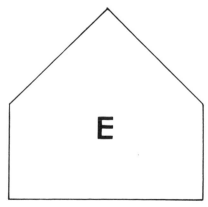

E

Candy Corn

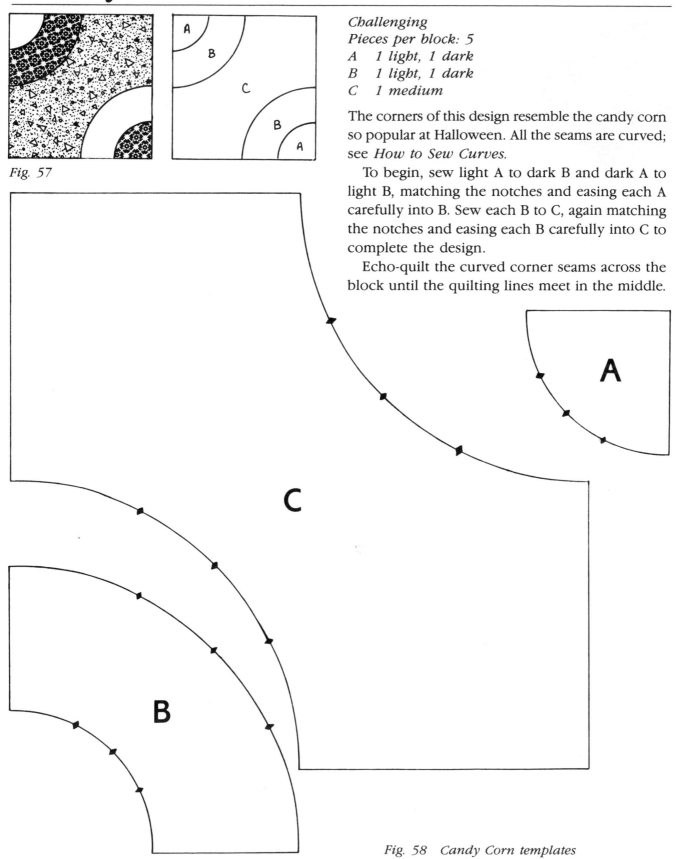

Fig. 57

Challenging
Pieces per block: 5
A   *1 light, 1 dark*
B   *1 light, 1 dark*
C   *1 medium*

The corners of this design resemble the candy corn so popular at Halloween. All the seams are curved; see *How to Sew Curves*.

To begin, sew light A to dark B and dark A to light B, matching the notches and easing each A carefully into B. Sew each B to C, again matching the notches and easing each B carefully into C to complete the design.

Echo-quilt the curved corner seams across the block until the quilting lines meet in the middle.

Fig. 58 *Candy Corn templates*

Corn & Beans

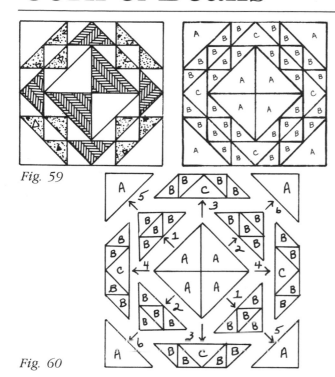

Fig. 59

Fig. 60

Moderate
Pieces per block: 44

A   6 light, 2 dark
B   20 light, 12 medium
C   4 dark

Why not make a project for the kitchen using this design? There is an exploded diagram to illustrate how to put this block together (Fig. 60). The templates are on page 32.

To begin, sew a light A to each dark A; sew the A-A triangles together to form the central square.

Next, sew 3 light B's around each of 4 medium B's, forming 4 right-angle triangles. Sew the long B-B edge of each to the central square.

For the outer pieced strips, sew a light B to each side of each C. Sew a medium B to each light B to form a straight strip. Sew to each edge of the central square.

Finally, sew an A to each medium B-B edge to complete the design.

Outline-quilt each medium and dark piece.

(Color Illus. 4B)

Spring Blossom

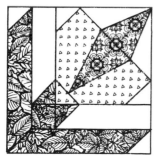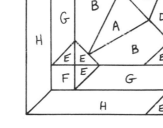

Fig. 61

Moderate
Pieces per block: 18

A	1 medium	E	4 light, 1 bright, 2 dark
B	1 bright, 1 bright reversed	F	1 dark
C	1 medium	G	1 light, 1 light reversed
D	1 light, 1 light reversed	H	1 dark, 1 dark reversed

Make this design 4 times, then turn the blocks so the tips of the flowers are all pointing towards the middle—interesting secondary effects will be created. Mitring is required at one corner; see *How to Mitre Corners.*

The templates are on page 32. To begin, sew a B to each side of A. Sew a bright E to the base of B-A-B; sew a light E to each short angled edge of B. Next sew a D to opposite edges of C, forming a right-angle triangle. Sew B-A-B to D-C-D.

Sew a dark E to each angled edge of G. Sew E-G to the left edge of the flower. Sew F to the remaining E-G strip, then sew to the base of the flower.

Sew a light E to each H as shown. Sew the E-H strips to the left and bottom edges of the block. Mitre the H-H corner to complete the design.

Outline-quilt the petals and leaves of the flower.

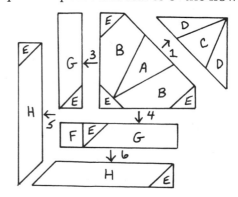

Fig. 62

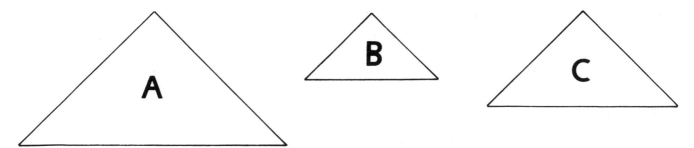

Fig. 63   Corn & Beans templates

Fig. 64   Spring Blossom templates

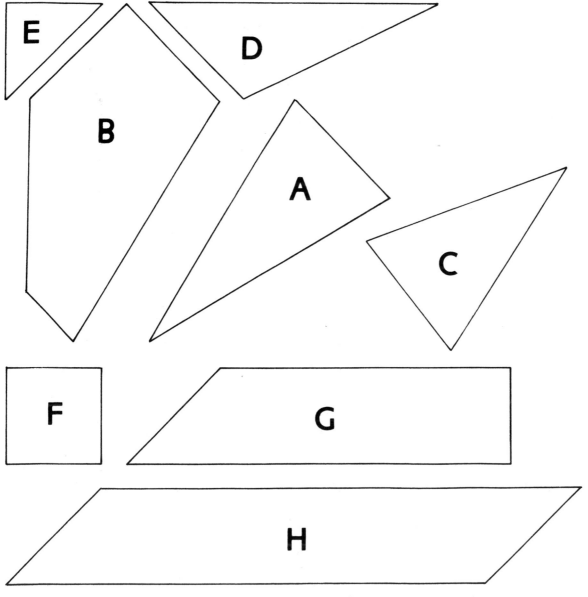

Illus. 1A.   This Treasure Box holds jewels, mementos, or other riches. Blocks of Flower Pot sparkle in contrast on a white background.

Illus. 1B.   This Jewelry Bag with Venerable Bede block is a portable holder for valuables on trips away.

Illus. 1C.   Small, easy-to-make Sachets will freshen storage areas with their potpourri scent. An element from Devil's Advocate is used.

*Illus. 2.   Sturdy denim-backed Picnic Blanket
& Cushions, together with Wine Tote and
Utensils Holder, make up a Picnic Set that will
enhance country outings with the family. Strips
of scrap fabric are used without any need for
templates, making this an extremely simple and
quick project.*

Illus. 3A (above).   Utensils Holder.

Illus. 3B (below).   Wine Tote.

B

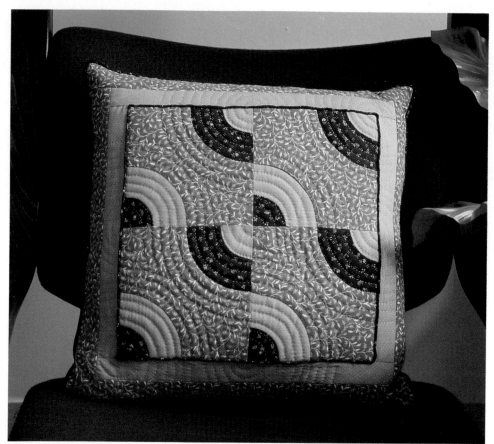

Illus. 4A. Patchwork pillows add color and coziness to your house, and will be warmly appreciated as housewarming gifts. Choose among the 4 styles shown or make them all! Pictured here: Square Pillow with Borders and Piping made up of 4 Candy Corn blocks and elaborately echo-quilted to enhance the overall design.

Illus. 4B. Oval Ruffled Pillow shown here uses 2 mirror-image blocks of Spring Blossom.

Illus. 5A. Whimsical pattern Dad's Ties uses real ties to make this example of the simple Square Pillow.

Illus. 5B. This Square Ruffled Pillow is sparked by the bright colors in 4 Tempest blocks.

E

Illus. 6.   This cheerful matched set of Oven Mitt, Patchwork Apron and Framed Pot Holder (featured in inset) will be an asset to any cook, with the appropriate choice of a block design. The choice here: English Thistle. The apron features a Seminole patchwork border.

F

Illus. 7A.   Patchwork in a Hoop uses an embroidery hoop to finish off the edges of the project and provide a hanger to display the work. Here, the name of the block, There's No Place Like Home, has been embroidered on to serve as a motto.

Illus. 7B.   Denim-lined Shoe Tote (here showing a Lancaster County block) provides an elegant solution to the problem of transporting a change of shoes to an exercise class or after-work function.

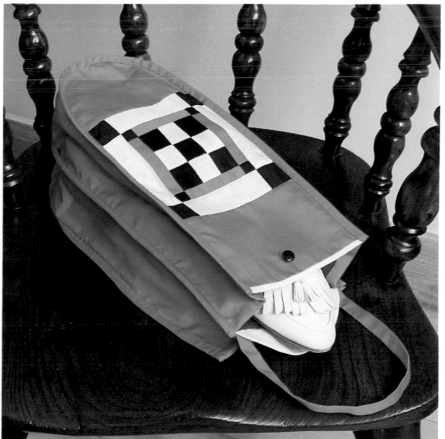

The Amish Quilt Carry-All organizes quilting equipment and makes it truly portable for travel or quilting meetings. Opposite sides of the Carry-All show Amish block designs and provide a chance to do some elaborate quilting on a small, manageable scale. Illus. 8A, left: Amish Bars. Illus. 8B, below: Amish Central Diamond.

Illus. 9.   When open the Amish Quilt Carry-All reveals pockets for books, stencils or patterns, thimble, thread, scissors, rotary cutter, pincushion, pencils and ruler, and fasteners for a hoop.

I

Illus. 10. This Geometric Wall Hanging is perfect for a narrow space in a hallway or along a stairway. The blocks pictured are Interlocked Squares (top); Interwoven Lines (middle); and Interlaced Star (bottom).

J

Illus. 11. A natural patchwork accessory for a desk, study or work area, this Letter Holder has a common theme in its 3 quilted blocks: Single Wedding Ring (top); Love in a Mist (middle); and Happy Marriage (bottom).

Illus 12A.   A perfect quilting companion, this Sewing Caddy folds up with a tie and has 2 large pockets inside to hold sewing equipment. The Waste Not quilt block is shown.

Illus 12B.   Sewing Caddy shown open over a chair arm, ready for use.

L

Illus. 13. Granny's Basket is the choice of block pattern for this handy Tote Bag. Fabric is pieced into long strips to make the braided handles.

Illus. 14A (above). A cozy Kitchen Set, featuring a trio of appliance covers. Left, Toaster Cover with Dutch Treat block; middle, Blender Cover with Jeroboam block; and right, Tea Cozy with Roundabout block.

Illus. 14B (below). Sunrise blocks in yellow and red make this Table Centerpiece a bright, sunny choice for the breakfast table.

N

Illus. 15A (above). Pot Holders are fast and easy to make, and excellent both as gifts and charity sale items. Top: Framed Pot Holder with Cups & Saucers block. Bottom: Round Pot Holder with Broken Sugar Bowl block.

Illus. 15B (below). Tray Cloth, made of 2 Devil's Advocate blocks, is one of many quilting projects for the kitchen.

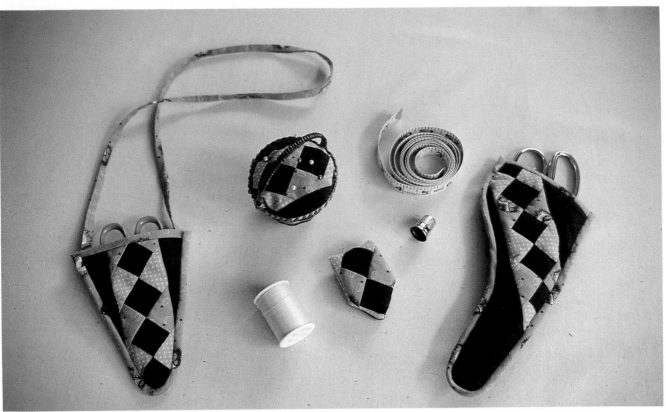

Illus. 16A.   This Sewing Set uses Seminole patchwork strips for its decoration. From left to right: Necklace Case for Scissors, Basket Pincushion, Needle Case, and Padded Case for 8-Inch Shears.

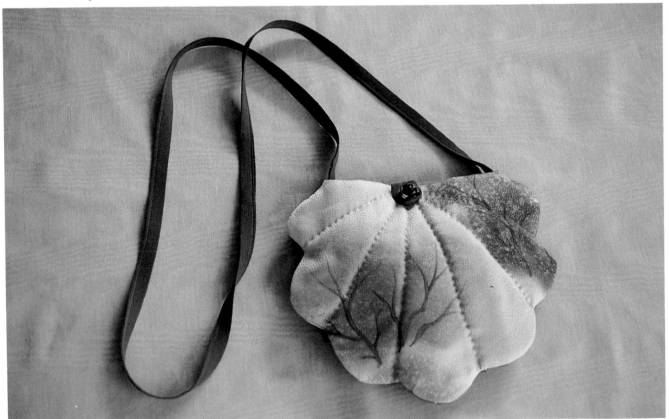

Illus. 16B.   An Evening Bag made up in a delicate fabric and quilted makes a stylish gift or accent note for your own wardrobe.

Country Farm

Fig. 65

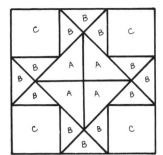

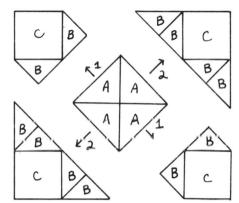

Fig. 66

Easy
Pieces per block: 20
A   2 bright, 2 medium
B   8 light, 4 dark
C   4 dark

You'll finish this simple design in no time! It is composed of 2 triangles sewn to each side of a central diagonal strip. Templates are on page 35.

Make the central diagonal strip first. Sew each bright A to a medium A. Sew the A-A triangles together, alternating fabrics, to make the central square. Sew a light B to adjacent edges of 2 dark C's. Sew each B-B edge thus made to opposite sides of the central A square.

For each of the triangles, sew a light B to adjacent edges of the remaining 2 C's; sew a dark B to each light B as shown.

Sew the triangles to each side of the central diagonal strip to complete the design.

Quilt the block to emphasize the star; then quilt 2 crisscrossing lines across the entire block.

Lancaster County

(Color Illus. 7B)

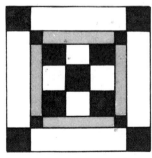

Fig. 67

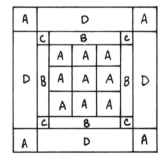

Easy
Pieces per block: 25

A 4 light, 9 dark	C 4 dark
B 4 medium	D 4 light

Those familiar with Amish designs will recognize many traditional elements in this block. When starkly contrasting colors are used, the finished result can be spectacular—it is also very quick to piece.

The templates are on page 35. To begin, sew the A pieces together in 3 rows with 3 squares in each row, alternating colors as shown in the diagram. Sew the rows together, matching seams carefully, to complete the middle.

Sew a B to each side of the middle. Sew a C to each end of the 2 remaining B's; sew to the top and bottom of the middle.

Sew a D to each side of the middle. Sew an A to each end of the remaining 2 D's; sew to the top and bottom of the middle to complete the design.

Outline-quilt all the medium and dark pieces.

33

Cross of Courage

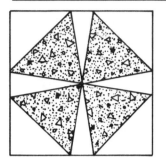
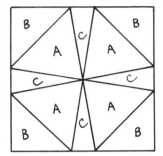

Fig. 68

Moderate
Pieces per block: 12
A   4 light
B   4 dark
C   4 dark

Striking and simple in appearance, this design has 8 seams, all meeting in the middle—careful marking and sewing are required.

To begin, sew each A to B, matching the dots. Arrange the A-B pieces alternately with the C's as shown in the diagram, then divide the block in half along one of the straight diagonal seams. Sew the C's to the A's in each half. Sew the halves together, matching seams carefully, to complete the design.

Outline-quilt the cross. Echo-quilt additional lines within the cross.

Happy Marriage

(Color Illus. 11)

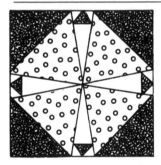
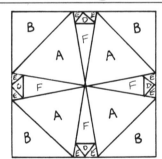

Fig. 69

Challenging
Pieces per block: 24

A	4 bright		E	4 dark, 4 dark
B	4 dark			reversed
D	4 light		F	4 dark

Because of the small pieces and 8 seams meeting in the middle, this design is a bit of a challenge. Mark the dots on A and B and the crosses on D and E carefully to avoid confusion.

To begin, sew each A to B, matching the dots. Sew an E to opposite edges of each D, matching the marked crosses. Sew the remaining edge of each D to F.

Arrange the A-B pieces alternately with the D-E-F pieces as shown in the diagram, then divide in half along one of the straight diagonal seams. Sew the E-F edges to the A's in each half. Sew the halves together, matching seams carefully, to complete the design.

Outline-quilt every seam.

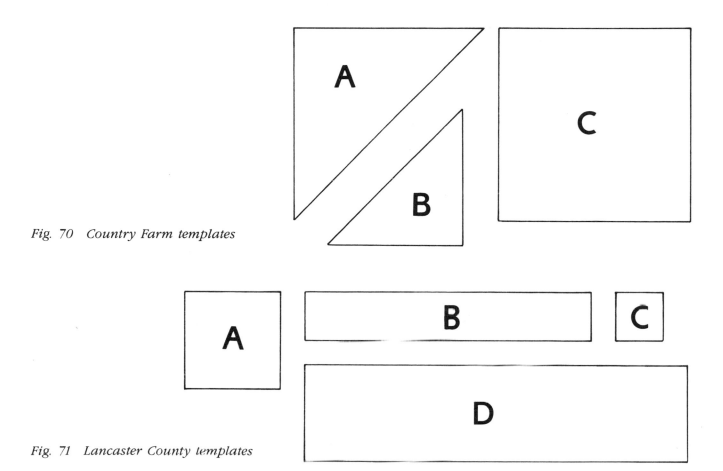

Fig. 70 Country Farm templates

Fig. 71 Lancaster County templates

Fig. 72 Cross of Courage and Happy
Marriage combined templates

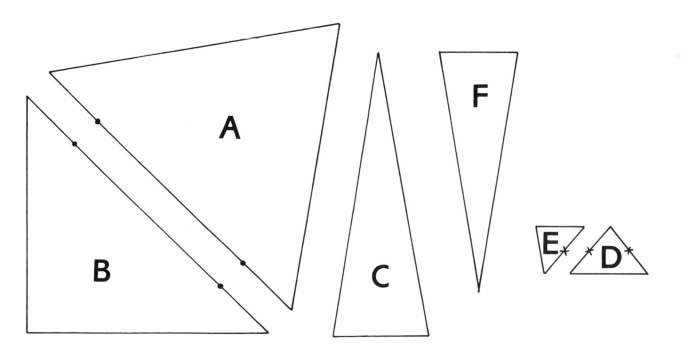

Broken Dishes

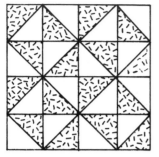

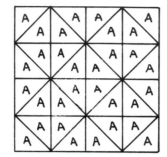

Fig. 73

Fig. 74   Broken Dishes template

Easy
Pieces per block: 32
A   16 light, 16 dark

A good beginner's block, Broken Dishes is composed of 16 pieced squares. Try to find 2 highly contrasting fabrics for a dramatic result.

The single template is at left. To begin, sew each light A to a dark A. Arrange the pieced squares in 4 rows, with 4 squares in each row, as shown in the diagram. Sew the squares together in rows, then sew the rows together, matching seams carefully, to complete the design.

To continue the idea of broken dishes, quilt a diagonal line across each pieced square in the direction opposite the seamline.

Broken Sugar Bowl

(Color Illus. 15A)

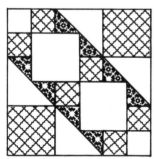

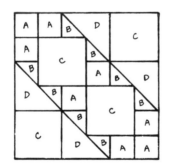

Fig. 75

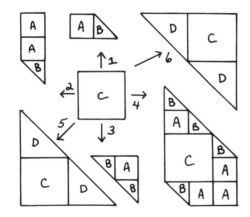

Fig. 76

Moderate
Pieces per block: 24

A 2 light, 6 bright	*C 2 light, 2 bright*
B 8 dark	*D 4 light*

If you make 4 of these blocks and set them end-to-end, you can create a marvelous cross-shaped design or strong diagonals—depending upon the way that you turn the blocks. The design is composed of 2 triangles sewn to each side of a central diagonal strip. The templates are on page 38.

Begin with the central diagonal strip. First for the upper left corner, sew a light and bright A together; sew a B to the bright A as shown. Next, sew a bright A to B; sew to left edge of C; sew A-A-B to the top edge of C. Next, sew two B's to adjacent edges of a bright A; sew to the third edge of C as shown. The first half of the central diagonal strip is complete; repeat this procedure for the second half, then sew the halves together.

For the triangles, sew D's to adjacent edges of the remaining C's, forming 2 right triangles. Sew the triangles to each side of the central diagonal strip to complete the design.

Outline-quilt the light and dark pieces.

Cups & Saucers

(Color Illus. 15A)

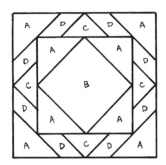

Fig. 77

Easy

Pieces per block: 21		*C*	*4 medium*
A	*4 bright, 4 dark*	*D*	*4 light, 4 light*
B	*1 medium*		*reversed*

A pretty, 3-dimensional effect is achieved when using highly contrasting fabrics. The block is assembled from the middle out. The templates are on page 38.

To begin, sew a dark A to each edge of B. Sew a D to each side of C, being sure to use reversed D's to keep each strip straight and even. Sew D-C-D to each dark A-A edge. Finally, sew a light A to each D-D edge to complete the design.

Outline-quilt all the pieces.

Jeroboam

(Color Illus. 14A)

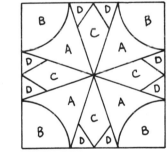

Fig. 78

Challenging

Pieces per block: 20		*C*	*4 dark*
A	*4 bright*	*D*	*4 light, 4 light*
B	*4 light*		*reversed*

This is not a beginner's block, so don't attempt it unless you are confident of your ability with curved seams and matching 8 seams at one central point. See *How to Sew Curves.*

The templates are on page 38. To begin, sew each A to B, easing B carefully into A. Sew a D to each short edge of C, matching the dots. Arrange the sewn pieces on a flat surface as shown in the diagram, then divide in half along one of the straight diagonal seams. Sew A-B to C-D in each half, then sew the halves together, matching seams carefully in the middle, to complete the design.

Outline-quilt the bright and dark pieces. Echo-quilt the curved edge of A across the A and B pieces every ½ inch or so.

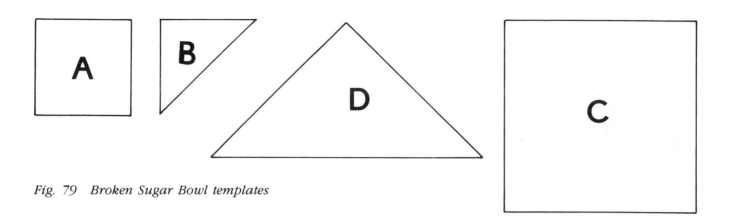

Fig. 79   Broken Sugar Bowl templates

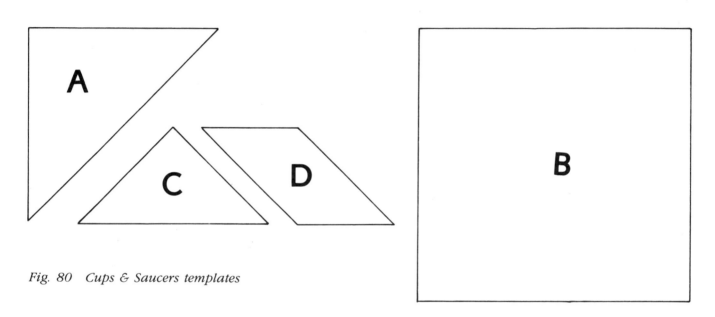

Fig. 80   Cups & Saucers templates

Fig. 81   Jeroboam templates

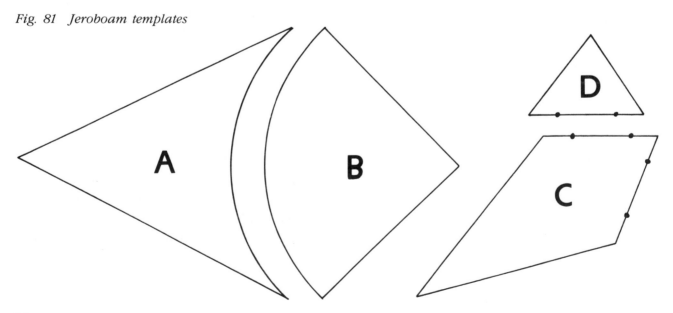

38

Dad's Ties

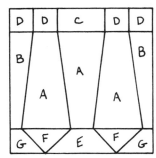

Fig. 82
Moderate
Pieces per block: 15

A	1 light, 1 bright, 1 medium	E	1 light
B	1 light, 1 light reversed	F	1 bright, 1 medium
C	1 light	G	1 light, 1 light reversed
D	2 light, 1 bright, 1 medium		

While eyeing my husband's large tie collection one day, I was inspired to design a patchwork block that would utilize those lovely fabrics in a whimsical way. I selected some ties I was sure he wouldn't want, but waited until he got home from work so I could receive permission to begin cutting. He was horrified with my idea, to say the least, but after much persuasion he grudgingly gave up 5 ties so

I could make the pillow shown in Color Illus. 5A. My suggestion to you is: don't ask permission—he'll never miss the ties. Or you can make up the design in cotton fabrics to avoid arguments!

If you do use tie fabrics, you must handle the patchwork pieces with care because most ties are cut on the bias, and pieces easily stretch out of shape. The finished result is worth the extra effort, however.

The templates are on page 40. To begin, sew a bright and medium A to each side of the light A. Sew a B to each A to complete the central strip.

Sew a bright and medium D to each side of C. Sew a light D to each end of the strip. Sew the D-C-D strip to the top of the central strip, matching seams and fabrics carefully.

For the bottom strip, sew an F to each side of E, matching the position of the fabrics to the A pieces. Sew a G to each F. Sew the bottom strip to the central strip to complete the design.

Outline-quilt each tie, then quilt a second line of stitching ½ inch away from the first around all edges of the ties. For a finishing touch, sew a small pearl or diamond "tie clip" to the middle of each tie.

Waste Not

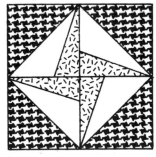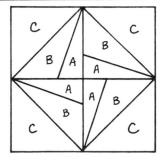

Fig. 83

Easy
Pieces per block: 12

A	4 dark
B	4 light
C	4 medium

This traditional block is always a delight because it epitomizes the essence of patchwork—not wasting any fabric!

The templates are on page 40. To make the large middle square, sew each A to a B. Sew 2 pairs of the A-B triangles together to form each half of the square. Sew the halves together, matching seams carefully, to complete the square.

Sew a C triangle to each edge of the square to complete the design.

Outline-quilt the medium and dark pieces.

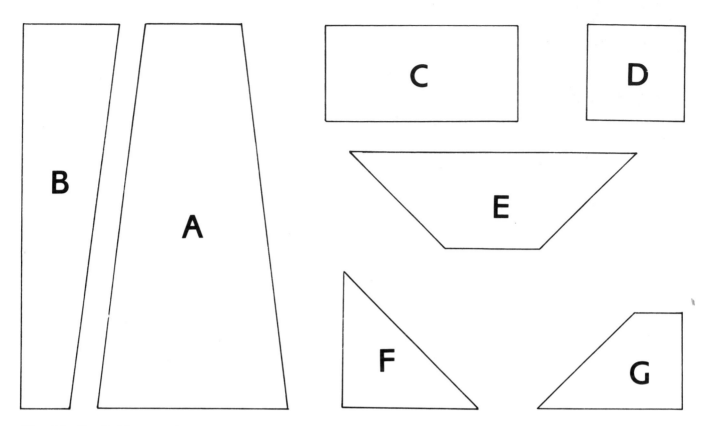

Fig. 84   *Dad's Ties templates*

Fig. 85   *Waste Not templates*

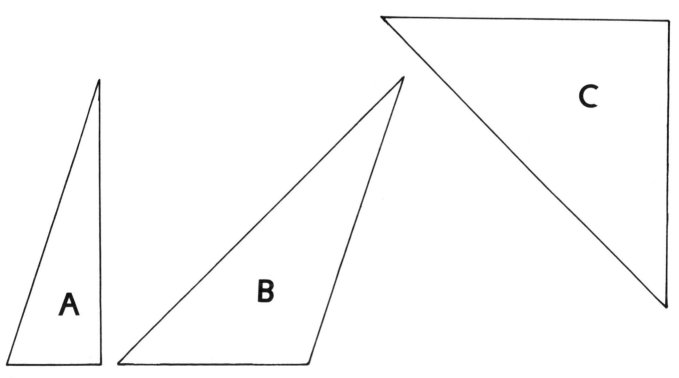

40

Deco Flower

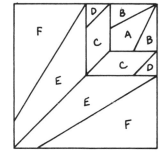

Fig. 86

Challenging
Pieces per block: 11

A   1 dark
B   1 light, 1 light
    reversed
C   1 medium, 1
    medium reversed

D   2 light
E   1 bright, 1
    bright reversed
F   1 light, 1 light
    reversed

Evoking an Art Deco feeling, this block requires insetting; see *How to Inset*.

The templates are on page 42. To begin, sew a B to each long edge of A. Sew a D to each outer edge of C; sew each E to an F. Sew C-D to each E as shown in the diagram, then sew the E-C seam. Inset A-B into the angle formed by the C's to complete the design.

Outline-quilt the leaves and petals of the flower.

English Thistle

(Color Illus. 6)

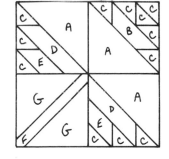

Fig. 87

Moderate
Pieces per block: 23

A   2 light, 1 bright
B   1 light
C   11 light, 1 bright
D   1 medium, 1
    medium reversed

E   1 medium, 1
    medium reversed
F   1 medium
G   2 light

Elegant and appealing, this block will enhance any project on which it is used. It is assembled easily enough in 4 squares; the tricky part is to get the F piece in the correct position in the middle—take extra care when piecing this area. The templates are on page 42.

To begin, sew a light C to both angled edges of B; sew C-B-C to the bright A. Sew three light C's to each edge of the bright C, forming a right-angle triangle. Sew to the C-B-C edge, forming the first square.

Sew a C to each D. Then sew C-D to each of the remaining A's. Following the diagram carefully, sew a C to adjacent edges of each E, forming a right-angle triangle. Sew the piece just made to D-C. Sew a G to each side of F.

Arrange the squares as shown in the diagram. Sew 2 pairs together for each half of the design; press the seam allowances in opposite directions. Sew the halves together, matching the seam in the middle, to complete the design.

Outline-quilt the medium and bright pieces.

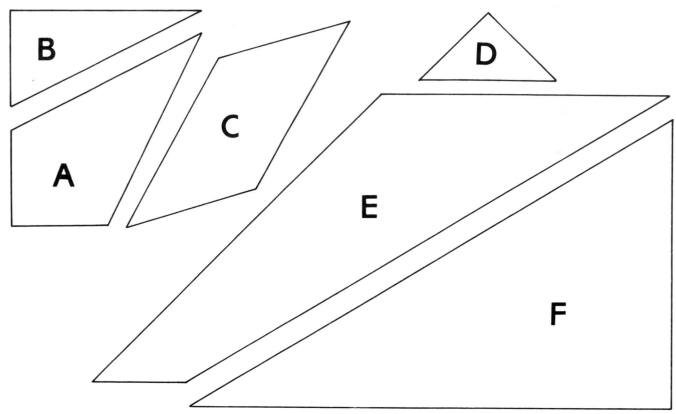

Fig. 88   Deco Flower templates

Fig. 89   English Thistle templates

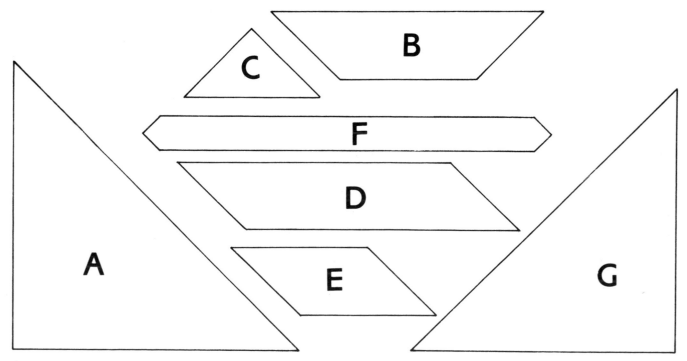

Love in a Mist

(Color Illus. 11)

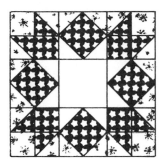

Fig. 90

Moderate
Pieces per block: 45

A   4 dark
B   8 light, 16
    bright, 8 dark

D   1 light
E   4 bright, 4 dark

The double star effect leaves one feeling as if the central star is seen through a mist—I suppose that's where the name of this traditional block came from. The design is assembled in squares.

To begin, sew 2 light and 2 bright B's to each A as shown in the diagram, forming 4 squares.

For each corner square, sew 2 pairs of bright and dark B's together, forming 2 squares. Arrange the B-B squares with a bright and dark E to form the larger pieced square shown. Stitch each E to a B-B square, then sew the halves together, matching seams carefully.

Arrange the squares in 3 rows with 3 squares in each row, following the diagram for position. Sew the squares together in rows, then sew the rows together, matching seams carefully, to complete the design.

Outline quilt the outer edges of the central star, then quilt the outer edges of the larger star.

Single Wedding Ring

(Color Illus. 11)

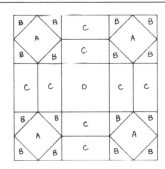

Fig. 91

Easy
Pieces per block: 29

A   4 light
B   16 dark

C   4 bright, 4 dark
D   1 light

This simple design is quick and easy to construct. Use highly contrasting fabrics to produce a strong ring effect in the middle.

Make each of the corner squares first by sewing a B to each edge of the A's. Next, sew each bright C to a dark C.

Arrange the squares in rows with 3 squares in each row as shown in the diagram. Sew together in rows, then sew the rows together, matching seams carefully, to complete the design.

Outline-quilt the inner and outer edges of the ring, then quilt around the remaining dark triangles.

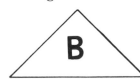

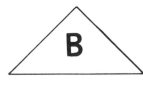

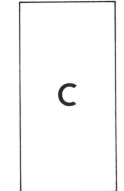

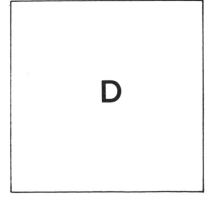

Fig. 92 Love in a Mist
and Single Wedding Ring
combined templates

Dutch Treat

(Color Illus. 14A)

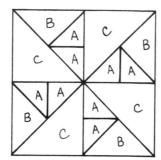

Fig. 93

Easy
Pieces per block: 16
A   4 light, 4 dark
B   4 light
C   4 striped

Use a striped fabric to enhance the twirling pinwheel effect. The block is assembled in 4 squares.

To make each square, sew a light A to a dark A, forming a right-angle triangle. Sew B to each dark A as shown in the diagram. Sew A-B to C.

Sew 2 pairs of squares together for each half of the design, sewing each A-A edge to a C edge. Sew the halves together to complete the design.

Outline-quilt the dark A pieces. Quilt the C pieces to emphasize the striped fabric.

Contrary Wife

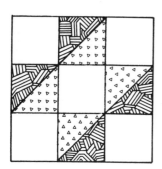

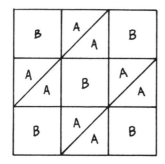

Fig. 94

Easy
Pieces per block: 13
A   4 medium, 4 dark
B   5 light

Simple yet appealing, this is an excellent block for a beginner to try. It is assembled in 3 rows with 3 squares in each row. The templates are given in 2 sizes—one for a 6-inch square, and one for a 12-inch square.

To begin, sew each medium A to a dark A, forming 4 pieced squares. Arrange these squares in 3 rows, alternating with the B's as shown in the diagram.

Sew the squares together in rows, then sew the rows together, matching seams carefully, to complete the design.

Outline-quilt the medium and dark pieces, then quilt a diagonal line across each B piece at the opposite angle to the A seams.

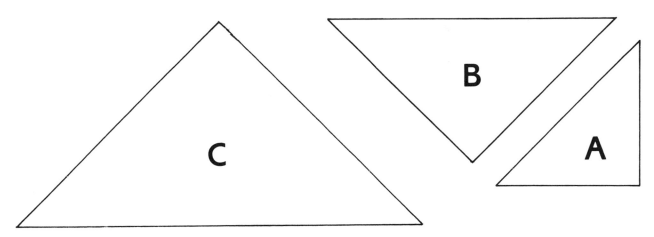

Fig. 95   Dutch Treat templates

Fig. 96   Contrary Wife templates

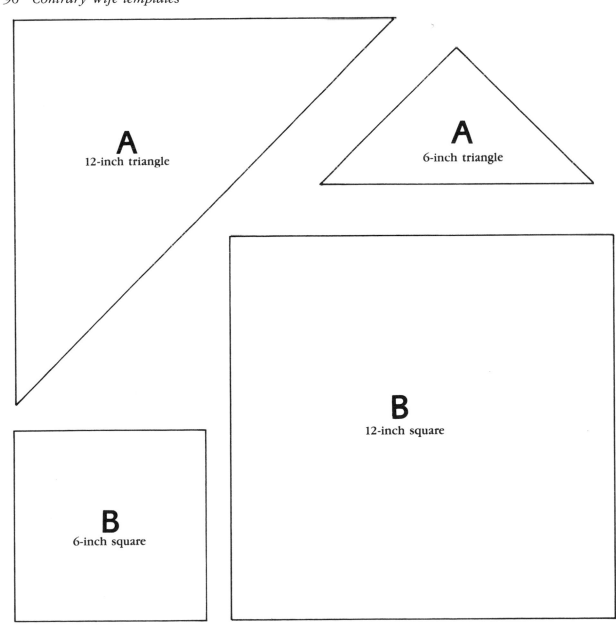

Which Way?

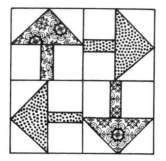
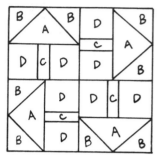

Fig. 97

Easy
Pieces per block: 24

A	2 medium, 2 dark	C	2 medium, 2 dark
B	8 light	D	8 light

For those, like me, who have trouble with map reading and directions, this would be an ideal block to make and feature on a tote bag, sewing caddy or jewelry bag. It is easily constructed in 4 squares. The templates are on page 48.

To begin, sew a B to adjacent edges of each A. Sew a D to opposite sides of each C. Matching the A and C fabrics, sew each D-C-D to an A to complete each square.

Arrange the arrows in a clockwise direction as shown in the diagram. Sew 2 pairs together for each half; then sew the halves together, matching seams carefully, to complete the design.

Outline-quilt each arrow.

Quandary

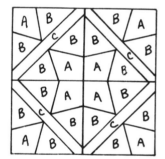

Fig. 98

Moderate
Pieces per block: 28

A 4 medium, 4 dark
B 8 light, 8 light reversed
C 4 striped

Connect 4 or more of these blocks end-to-end and you'll create a wonderful maze with strong diagonals darting through it. The block is easily assembled in 4 squares—just be sure to mark the dots on the A and B pieces to prevent confusion about which edge to sew. The templates are on page 48.

Each square is constructed in the same way. Sew a B to each long edge of A, matching the dots and forming a right-angle triangle. Sew matching A-B triangles to each side of C.

Arrange the squares on a flat surface as shown in the diagram. Sew 2 pairs of squares together to make each half of the design; sew the halves together, matching seams carefully, to complete the design.

Outline-quilt the A and C pieces.

Twist

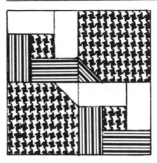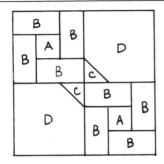

Fig. 99

Moderate
Pieces per block: 14
A   2 light
B   4 bright striped,
*   4 dark striped*
C   1 bright striped,
*   1 dark striped*
D   2 light

Striped fabrics are often ignored in patchwork, and unjustly so! Lovely 3-dimensional effects can be created by the cunning use of stripes. You must be careful to match the stripes, however, or the result can be ruined. You can, of course, use plain or printed fabrics for this block as well as stripes.

The block is assembled in 4 squares. The templates are on page 48.

Begin with the A-B square. With right sides facing and one edge flush, stitch B to A from the flush edge to halfway across A; stop your stitching and press. Stitch the second B to the flush A-B edge. Continue in a clockwise direction for the third and fourth B's in the same manner. Go back to the first unfinished seam; you have now created a flush edge to which the first B can be sewn. Finish that seam. Repeat for the second A-B square.

Sew each C to D to complete the other 2 squares. Following the diagram carefully, sew each A-B square to a C-D square for each half. Sew the halves together, matching stripes and seams carefully, to complete the design.

Quilt the outline of each "twist"; then quilt along the stripes to emphasize the twist.

Roundabout

(Color Illus. 14A)

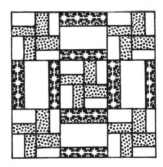

Fig. 100

Easy
Pieces per block: 52
A   4 light, 8 bright, 8 medium, 20 dark
B   4 light
C   4 bright, 4 medium

While there are a lot of pieces to this design, the shapes are all very simple and easy to sew. If you have a rotary cutter, now is the time to use it— you can cut out the A pieces very quickly and efficiently by using a cutter on multiple layers of fabric. Even if you don't have a rotary cutter, mark

long 1-inch strips (which includes seam allowance) across the width of your fabric, then divide into 1½-inch A pieces and 2½-inch C pieces. The B's can be cut in a similar way. The templates are on page 48.

To begin, arrange all the pieces on a flat surface as shown in the diagram, then divide into A squares and B-C squares. For each A square, sew 4 pairs of A pieces together, then to each other to create the pinwheel effect. Sew a C to each edge of B for the B-C squares.

Arrange the pieced squares in 3 rows with 3 squares in each row. Sew the squares together in rows, then sew the rows together, matching seams carefully, to complete the design.

Outline-quilt each dark A pinwheel, then quilt around each B piece.

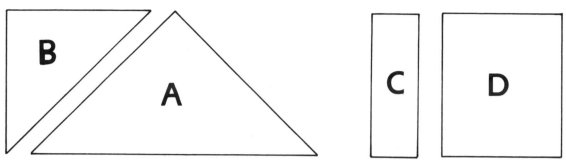

Fig. 101   *Which Way? templates*

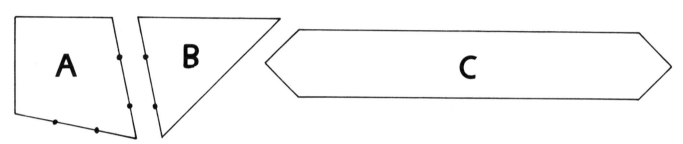

Fig. 102   *Quandary templates*

Fig. 103   *Twist templates*

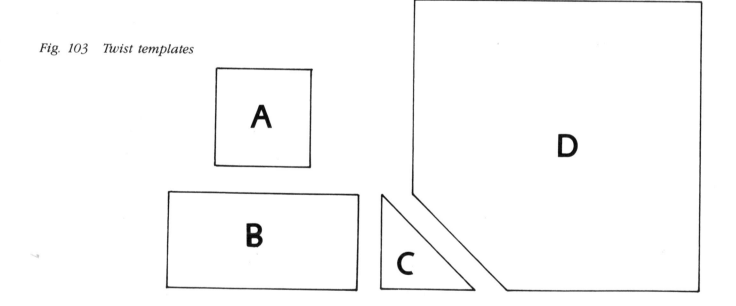

Fig. 104   *Roundabout templates*

Tempest

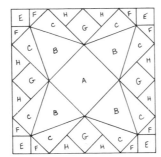

Fig. 105

Challenging
Pieces per block: 37

A	1 dark	E	4 dark
B	4 bright	F	8 medium
C	4 light, 4 light reversed	G	4 dark
		H	8 medium

A slightly more complex version of Turbulence, Tempest creates an optical illusion of depth when a very dark fabric is used for the square pieces. The block is assembled as a central diagonal strip flanked by 2 large triangles. The templates are on page 50.

To make the central diagonal strip, sew a C to opposite edges of 2 B's. Sew the remaining edge of each B to opposite sides of A. Make 2 right-angle triangles by sewing 2 F's each to adjacent edges of 2 E's as shown in the diagram. Sew F-F to each C-C edge.

For each triangle, sew a C to opposite edges of the 2 remaining B's. Make 2 E-F triangles as described above and sew each F-F to a C-C edge. Sew 2 H's to adjacent edges of each G, forming 4 right-angle triangles. Sew a G-H edge to each C to complete the triangle.

Sew a triangle to each side of the central diagonal strip to complete the design. Be sure to match seams carefully when pinning.

Quilt around the central star, then quilt to emphasize the dark squares.

Turbulence

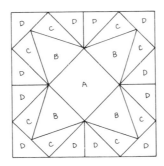

Fig. 106

Moderate
Pieces per block: 25

A	1 dark	C	4 dark, 4 dark reversed
B	4 bright	D	8 light, 4 dark

Use highly contrasting fabrics for a dramatic effect. The block is assembled as a central diagonal strip flanked by 2 large triangles. The templates are on page 50.

To make the central diagonal strip, sew a C to opposite edges of 2 B's. Sew the remaining edge of each B to opposite sides of A. Sew a dark D to each C-C edge.

For each triangle, sew a C to opposite edges of the 2 remaining B's. Sew a dark D to each C-C edge. Sew 4 pairs of light D's together, making 4 right-angle triangles. Sew one D-D triangle to each C to complete the large triangle.

Sew a triangle to each side of the central diagonal strip, matching seams carefully, to complete the design.

Quilt around the bright and dark pieces.

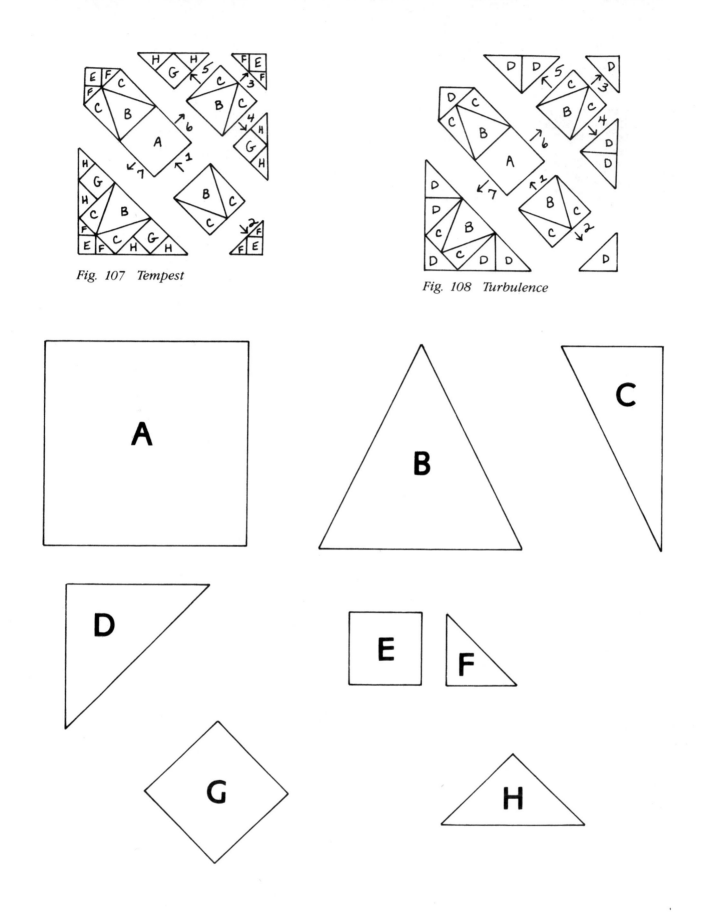

Fig. 107 Tempest

Fig. 108 Turbulence

Fig. 109 Tempest and Turbulence combined templates

Flower Pot

 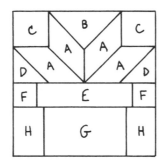

Fig. 110

Challenging
Pieces per block: 15

A	2 bright, 2 bright reversed	E	1 dark
B	1 light	F	2 light
C	2 light	G	1 dark
D	2 light	H	2 light

Derived from a Pennsylvania Dutch folk-art design, Flower Pot is a cheerful, uncompromising pattern. Insetting is required along the top edge of the block: see *How to Inset*.

To begin, sew each A to its reverse, making 2 pairs of petals. Sew the petals together along the central seam as shown. Inset B in between the middle petals; inset a C in each corner. Sew a D to the side edge of each A to complete the flower section.

For the pot, sew an F to each end of E. Sew an H to each side of G. Sew F-E-F to H-G-H to complete the pot.

Sew the flower section to the pot to complete the design.

Outline-quilt the pot and each flower petal.

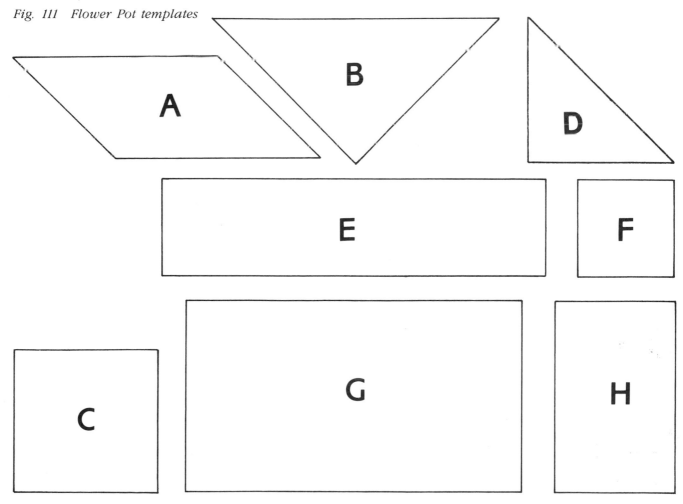

Fig. 111 Flower Pot templates

Granny's Basket

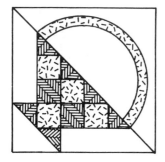
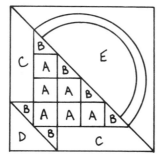

Fig. 112

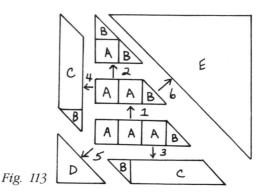

Fig. 113

Moderate
Pieces per block: 17

A	4 medium, 2 dark
B	6 dark
C	1 light, 1 light reversed
D	1 light
E	1 light
F	1" × 9" strip of bias fabric

Baskets are perennial favorites among quilters, probably because the shape is so easily recognized. You've probably never seen this basket before, because it is an adaptation of several basket designs rolled into one! The piecing is very easy, but you'll need a bit of patience (and lots of pins and pressing) to get the handle perfect. Be *sure* the handle strip is cut on the bias! It is appliquéd in place; see *How to Appliqué*.

To begin with the bottom strip of the basket, sew a dark A between 2 medium A's; sew a B to the right end of this strip. Next, sandwich a medium A between a dark A and B; sew to the first pieced strip. Finally, make a right-angle triangle by sewing a B to 2 adjacent edges of A; sew to the second pieced strip to complete the basket shape.

Sew a B to the straight edge of each C; sew B-C to each side of the basket. Sew D to the base of the basket and sew E to the top. The piecing is now complete.

If desired, use a compass to lightly mark the position of the handle on the E piece. Press both long edges of the bias strip ¼ inch to the wrong side. Press one short end ¼ inch to the wrong side. Begin pinning the pressed short end of the handle to E, flush with one corner edge of the basket. Work your way around to the other edge, gently pulling, pressing, and pinning the bias strip as you go along. Do not despair—because it is cut on the bias, all ripples and wrinkles can eventually be eased out. When you reach the opposite end, trim away any excess, leaving ¼ inch to turn under. Turn the seam allowance under, flush with the top edge of the basket, and pin in place. Appliqué the handle to E with tiny stitches and matching thread.

Quilt around each edge of the handle and the edge of the basket, then outline-quilt each dark piece within the basket.

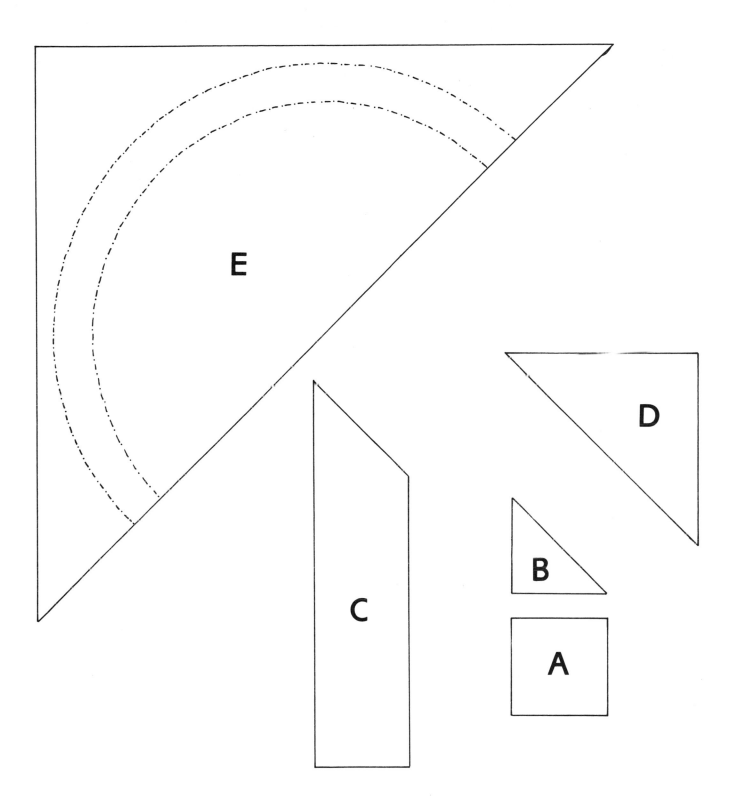

Fig. 114   Granny's Basket templates

Sunrise

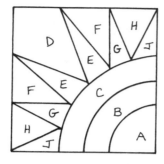

Fig. 115

Challenging
Pieces per block: 14

A 1 dark
B 1 medium
C 1 bright
D 1 light
E 1 dark, 1 dark
   reversed
F 1 light, 1 light
   reversed

G 1 medium, 1
   medium reversed
H 1 light, 1 light
   reversed
J 1 dark, 1 dark
   reversed

Challenging though this may be, you can expect a dazzling result if you take your time and mark the pieces carefully before beginning. The block contains 3 curved seams; see *How to Sew Curves*.

To begin, sew A to B, matching the notches and easing B carefully into A. Sew B to C, again matching notches and easing C into B. Press carefully.

For the pieced curve, sew E to each side of D, matching the dots. Sew F to E, matching the crosses. Sew G to F, matching the notches. Sew H to G, matching the open circles, and sew J to H, matching the diamonds. You should now have a curved edge to match the edge of C. Sew the pieced curve to C, matching the notches and easing carefully to fit. Press.

Echo-quilt the curved seam every ½-inch across the A, B, and C pieces. Outline-quilt each of the rays of the sun.

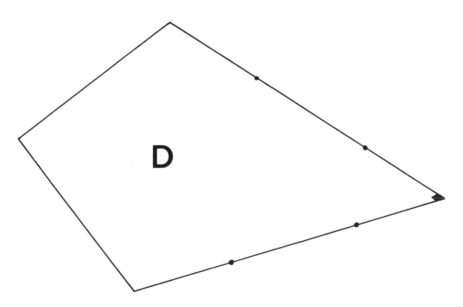

Fig. 116 Sunrise template

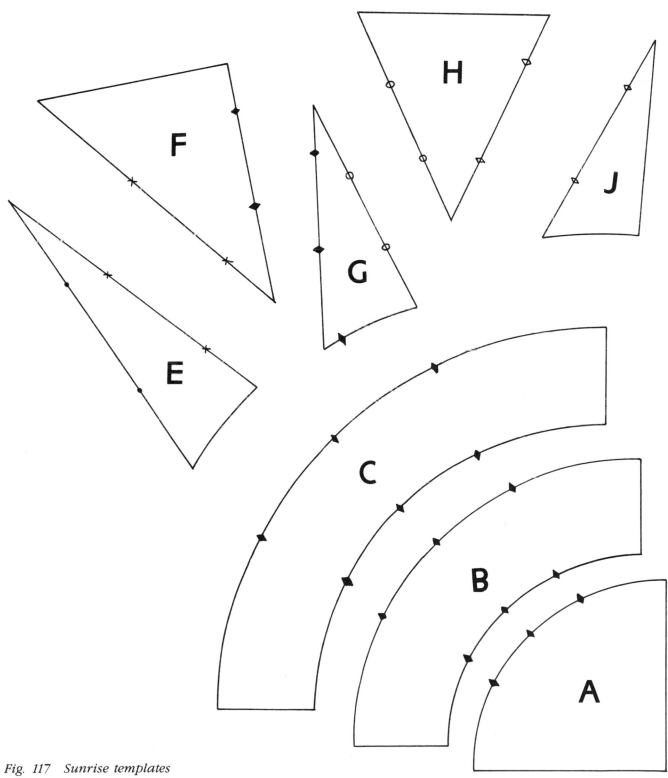

Fig. 117   Sunrise templates

Zephyr

 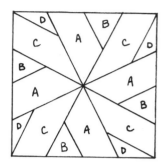

Fig. 118

Challenging
Pieces per block: 16

A	4 dark	C	4 medium
B	4 light	D	4 light

One feels that a gentle breeze would be enough to start this pinwheel spinning! It's a bit of a challenge to match up the 8 seams in the middle. Mark the pieces carefully to avoid confusion between the A and C pieces.

To begin, sew a B to each A, matching the dots. Sew a D to each C, matching the notches.

Arrange the pieces on a flat surface as shown in the diagram, then divide in half along a straight diagonal edge. Sew A-B to C in each half, matching the crosses. Also sew C-D to A where applicable.

Sew the halves together, matching seams carefully in the middle, to complete the design.

Outline-quilt each blade of the pinwheel.

Reflections

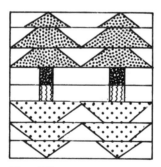

Fig. 119

Moderate
Pieces per block: 40

A	4 light I, 2 light II, 2 bright	D	4 light I, 4 light I reversed
B	2 light I, 4 light II, 4 bright	E	2 light I
		F	2 medium, 2 dark
C	2 light I, 2 light I reversed	G	4 light I

Use lighter shades of the same color for the 2 lower (reflecting) trees and trunks to simulate a real reflection on water. There are many pieces, but the block is easily assembled in 8 strips.

To begin with the top strip, sew a bright A to each side of a light I B; for the bottom strip, sew a light II A to each side of a light I B. Sew a C to each A to complete the strips.

For the central trunk strips, sew matching F's to each side of each E. Sew a G to each F; sew the strips just made together, matching seams carefully.

For the remaining 4 strips, sew a matching B to each side of each light I A; sew a D to each B. Sew 2 pairs of matching strips together. Sew the bright pair to the dark trunk strip; sew the light II pair to the medium trunk strip. Sew the matching top and bottom strips in place to complete the design.

Outline-quilt each tree and trunk.

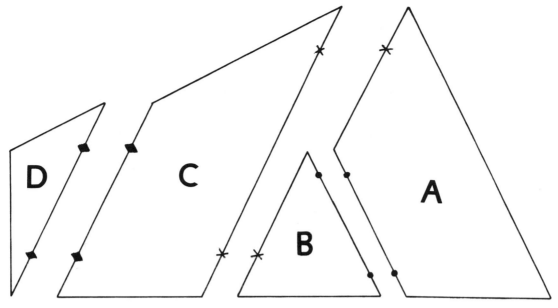

Fig. 120 Zephyr templates

Fig. 121 Reflections templates

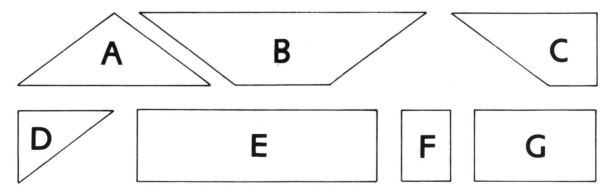

Venerable Bede

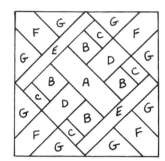

Fig. 122

Moderate
Pieces per block: 25

A	1 bright	E	2 light
B	4 medium	F	2 bright, 2 dark
C	4 light	G	8 medium
D	2 dark		

While visiting the tomb of the Venerable Bede (a religious scholar and writer, also known as the "Father of English History") in Durham Cathedral, England, I noticed a small woodcut on one of the benches and hastily drew a rough sketch on a scrap of paper. The sketch blossomed into this design, which I've named in honor of that great man. The block is composed of a big square edged with 4 triangles.

To begin, sew each B to a C. Sew B-C to each side of each D, keeping the C's aligned along the same edge. Sew B-D-B to each side of A. Sew E to each C-B-A-B-C edge to complete the central square.

To make each triangle, sew a G to opposite sides of each F. Aligning the bright F's with A, sew a G-F-G triangle to each E. Matching the seams of the dark pieces, sew the G-F-G triangles to each remaining edge of the central square.

Outline-quilt the light, bright and dark pieces.

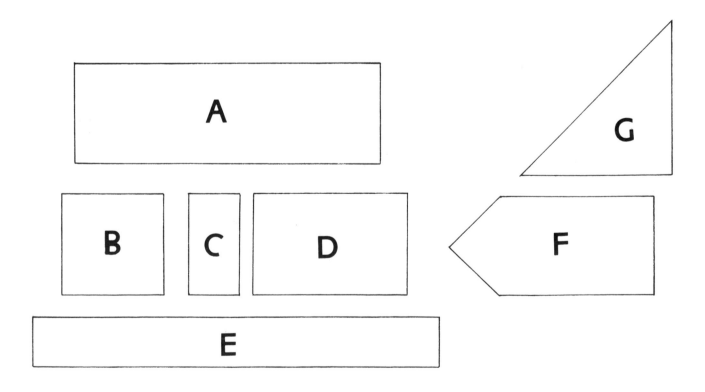

Fig. 123   Venerable Bede templates

There's No Place Like Home

(Color Illus. 7A)

Fig. 124
Easy
Pieces per block: 15

A	1 bright	F	1 medium
B	1 sky reversed	G	2 light, 2
C	1 medium		medium
	reversed	H	4 dark
D	1 sky reversed	J	1 dark
E	1 sky reversed		

Fig. 125   There's No Place Like Home templates

House designs are well loved by quilters and this simple one will add a feeling of warmth to any project. Make it in fabrics to match your own home!

To begin, sew B to the left edge of A. Sew D and E to opposite sides of C, then sew D-C-E to A. Sew A to F.

Sew each light G to a medium G. Sew an H to each edge of G-G. Sew H-G-H to each side of J to complete the bottom of the house, positioning the light G's along the same edge. Sew the bottom of the house to F along the light G edge to complete the design.

Outline-quilt the door, windows, roof, and chimney.

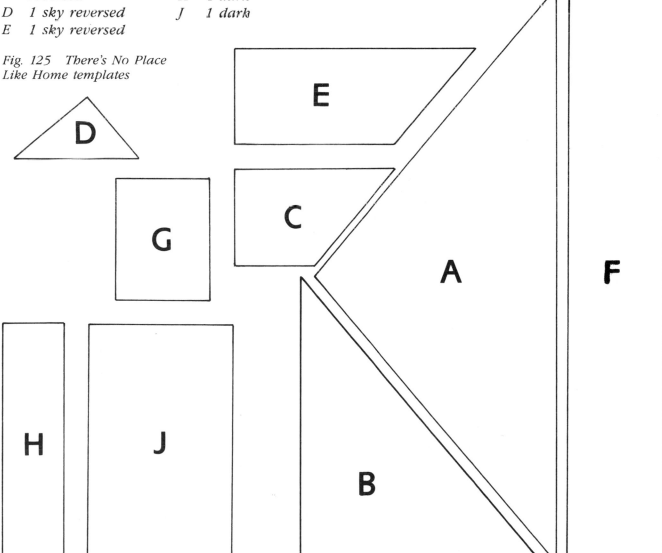

Small Quilting Projects

SEWING AIDS

Sewing Set

(Color Illus. 16A)

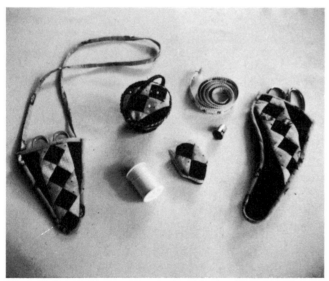

Fig. 126

Easy
Requirements
Fabrics: ⅛-yard bright, ⅜-yard medium,
¼-yard dark
Batting
Polyester fibrefill
Small wicker basket, about 3" diameter
Fabric glue
Fastener: snaps or Velcro

Try your hand at Seminole patchwork and create this handy Sewing Set for yourself or as a gift for a friend. It only took me a few hours to make all 4 pieces—the entire set can easily be made in an evening or two. If you have a rotary cutter, your job will be even faster, as rotary cutters are ideal for Seminole Patchwork. Be sure to press carefully between each step.

Before beginning, review the following sections: *Rotary Cutting, Assembling a Project for Quilting, Machine Quilting,* and *Binding a Project.*

SEMINOLE PATCHWORK
(The strips you make will be long enough to create all of the projects in this set.) Cut the following strips from the designated fabrics:
bright: 2" × 38"
medium: 2" × 38"
dark: 1½" × 38"
Sew the bright fabric to one long edge of the dark strip and the medium fabric to the other edge of the dark strip. Your pieced strip will resemble Figure 128. Next, using a ruler, measure and mark off 1½-inch-wide pieces across the entire strip; cut along each marked line. Following Figure 129, turn your pieces so the fabrics alternate. Sew the strips

together, matching the seams indicated by the arrows in Figure 130. Your pieced strip should look like Figure 131.

Using a ruler and pencil, draw a straight line across the top and bottom to eliminate the staggered edges; make sure the width of the piece you have marked is 2¼ inches (Fig. 131). Trim off the excess fabric along the marked lines. Press gently because the strip is now on the bias and will tend to stretch.

Your finished length should be approximately 34 inches. When cutting patchwork pieces from your strip, place the template in the middle of the strip; allow ¼-inch seam allowances around all edges.

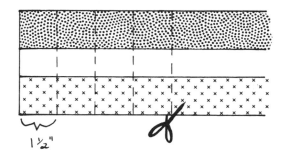

Fig. 128

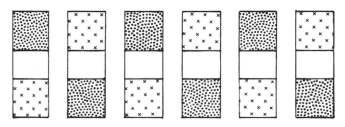

Fig. 129

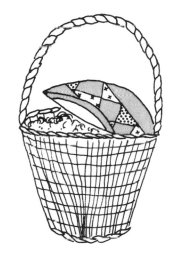

Fig. 127   Basket Pincushion

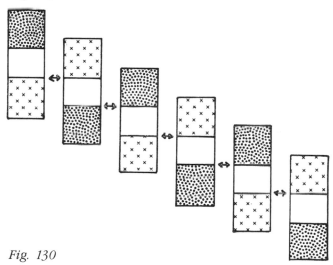

Fig. 130

BASKET PINCUSHION

Measure the diameter of the top of your basket; add ¾-inch to the measurement; use a compass to cut out a circular paper pattern to this measurement. Measure and mark a 1¾-inch-wide strip across the middle of your circular pattern. Cut the pattern into 3 pieces. Use the central strip to cut a piece of Seminole patchwork; use one of the side patterns to cut 2 pieces from the dark fabric. Be sure to add a ¼-inch seam allowance around the edges of all the pieces. Sew a side piece to each edge of the central strip. Machine-baste ¼-inch away from the edges of the pieced circle all around. Gently pull the basting to draw the edges of the circle to the same size as the opening of the basket.

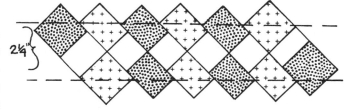

Fig. 131

If your basket is not tightly woven, you may wish to line the interior with a scrap of dark fabric. Stuff the basket with fibrefill until quite full.

Run a thin line of fabric glue around the inner top edge of the basket. Insert the gathered fabric into the basket, pressing the sides against the glue and making sure no raw edges or basting stitches show. Let dry before using.

Fig. 132   Needle Case

NEEDLE CASE

Cut a length of Seminole patchwork to match the piece shown in Figure 132; the length should be approximately 6 inches and the piece should include 4 complete dark squares plus a ¼-inch seam allowance at each pointed end. Use the piece as a pattern to cut a back from the bright fabric; also cut a piece of batting to the same size.

Baste the batting to the wrong side of the pieced front. Pin the front to the back with right sides facing and raw edges even. Beginning in the middle of one side edge, stitch the front to the back all around, turning your stitching sharply at the points and leaving a 1½-inch opening for turning. Turn to the right side. Fold the raw edges at the opening ¼-inch inside and slip-stitch the opening closed. Sew snaps or Velcro near each tip of the case to finish.

PADDED CASE FOR 8-INCH SHEARS

Trace separate templates for pieces A, B, C, and D. Cut the following pieces:

A   1 dark, 1 dark reversed
B   1 dark, 1 dark reversed
C   1 pieced strip, 1 pieced strip reversed
D   1 dark, 1 dark reversed, 2 batting
Bias binding: 1″ × 4¼″; 1″ × 20″

Arrange the cut pieces on a flat surface; position A, B, and C to create the front and back sections of the case. Sew A and C to opposite sides of each B.

Assemble each section of the case as directed in *Assembling a Project for Quilting*, using the dark D pieces for the backs. Machine-quilt along each edge of the patchwork strip; quilt around each dark square within the strip. Baste around the edges of each section.

See *Binding a Project*. Bind the straight top edge of each quilted section. Baste the sections together around the curved edges with wrong sides facing; bind the edges, folding the ends under neatly to finish.

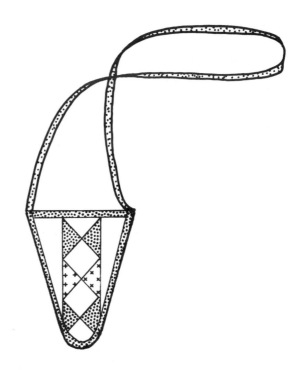

Fig. 133   Necklace Case for Small Scissors

NECKLACE CASE FOR SMALL SCISSORS

Trace separate templates for pieces E, F, and G. Cut the following pieces:

E   1 dark, 1 dark reversed
F   1 pieced strip
G   3 dark, 2 batting
Bias binding: 1″ × 4½″; 1″ × 13½″
Straight binding: 1″ × 30″

Sew an E to each side of F, keeping the top edges straight. The back section (G) of the case is not pieced.

See *Assembling a Project for Quilting*. Assemble the pieced top and one G (for the back section) as directed, using the remaining dark G pieces for the backs (or linings). Machine-quilt along each edge of the patchwork strip; quilt around each dark square. The back is not quilted. Baste around the edges of each section.

See *Binding a Project*. Bind the straight top edge of the front and back with the short bias strips. Baste the sections together around the curved edges with wrong sides facing; bind the edges with bias binding, folding the ends under neatly to finish.

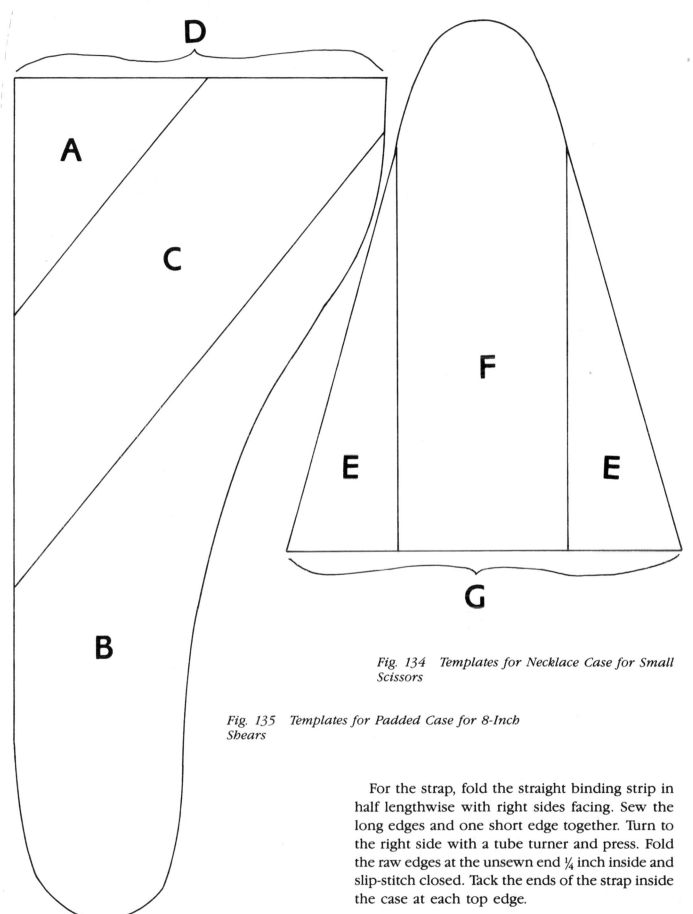

Fig. 134   Templates for Necklace Case for Small Scissors

Fig. 135   Templates for Padded Case for 8-Inch Shears

For the strap, fold the straight binding strip in half lengthwise with right sides facing. Sew the long edges and one short edge together. Turn to the right side with a tube turner and press. Fold the raw edges at the unsewn end ¼ inch inside and slip-stitch closed. Tack the ends of the strap inside the case at each top edge.

Sewing Caddy

Fig. 135

Fig. 136

Most needleworkers are so busy making projects for other people that they rarely create anything for themselves. This very quick and easy project will enable you to organize all your sewing equipment in a neat little package that can be carried with you wherever you go. For your convenience, the sewing caddy has been designed to rest over the arm of a chair during use; it has 2 large pockets that can be filled with all your sewing necessities.

Many thanks to Lisa Benjamin of London, England, who has graciously allowed me to use her original design in this book.

Easy
Finished size: About 6" × 7"
Requirements
Pieced blocks: 4 6" squares—scraps or ⅛ yard each of 3 to 5 fabrics
Ties: 2 1" × 12"—fabric scrap
Piping cord: ¼" diameter—¾ yard length
Piping strips: 4 1" × 6½"—fabric scrap
Fabric strip*: 2½" × 6½"—scrap of matching fabric
Back: 1 6½" × 26½"—¼ yard matching fabric (includes fabric for binding)
Batting: 1 6" × 26"
Binding: 2 1" × 6½"; 2 1" × 15"

*Measure the width of the arm of your favorite chair; if the measurement is wider than 2", adjust the width of the fabric strip accordingly.

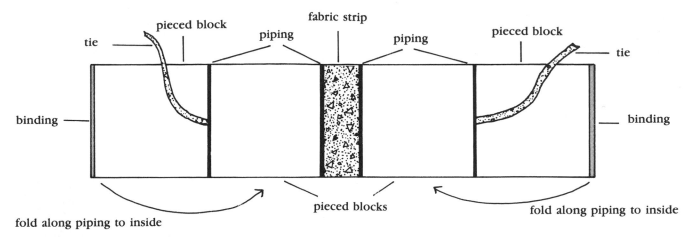

Fig. 137 Outside of Sewing Caddy

Instructions: Select 1 to 4 of the 6-inch square block designs. Piece 4 blocks as directed in the individual instructions.

For the ties, fold the fabric strips in half lengthwise, stitch the long edge and one short edge of each. Turn to the right side using a tube turner; press. With raw edges even, baste a tie to the middle of the right edge of one block and the left edge of another.

Cut the piping into 4 pieces, each 6½-inches long. Review *Piping* for instructions on making and attaching the piping; cover each length of piping cord with a piping strip. Attach the piping to the right and left edges of the 2 pieced blocks with ties, sandwiching a tie between the piping and the block on each.

Sew the 2½" × 6½" fabric strip between the 2 piped blocks, along the edges without the ties. Sew the remaining pieced blocks to the piped edges of the first 2 blocks, along the edges with the ties.

See *Assembling a Project for Quilting*; assemble the project as directed. Quilt each of the blocks by hand or machine following the individual instructions. See *Binding a Project*; bind each short side-edge of the quilted piece with a 6½-inch length of binding fabric.

Fold the 2 outer blocks to the inside along the piping as shown in the diagram. Baste in place along the top and bottom edges. Bind the remaining raw edges of the project with the long strips of binding fabric, folding under the corners edges to finish neatly. Remove the basting.

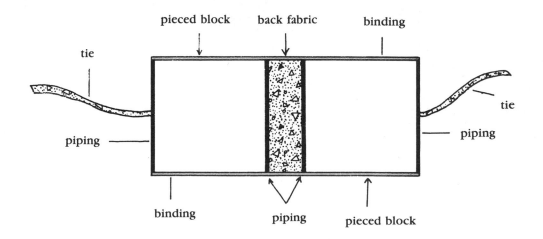

Fig. 138 Inside of Sewing Caddy (after folding)

Amish Quilt Carry-All

(Color Illus. 8A, 8B, and 9)

Fig. 139

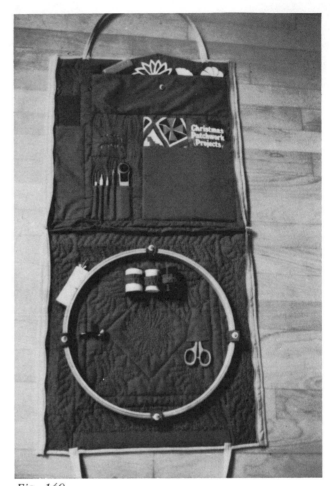

Fig. 140

Fig. 141

Do you find yourself rushing off to quilt meetings and workshops carrying all your equipment in a nondescript sack, or worse, a plastic bag? Then, when you reach your destination, how often have you forgotten to bring your thimble, or a ruler, or a pair of scissors? This Amish Quilt Carry-All will not only organize all your quilting supplies in one portable place, it will give you the chance to show off your piecing and quilting skills to those who are really interested—your fellow quilters!

While technically this project can be made very quickly (if you quilt by machine), I would advise you to take your time and do some splendid hand quilting. The 2 Amish designs given here lend themselves beautifully to intricate quilting. Make the same block twice, or do as I did and make a different block for each side of the bag using co-ordinating fabrics.

Moderate
Finished size: 19" square
Requirements
Pieced blocks: 2 19" square—⅜ yard light, ⅜ yard bright, ¼ yard dark
Back: 2 19½" square—1¼ yards medium fabric (includes fabric for all interior pieces and pieced blocks)

Batting: 2 19" square
Remainder of bag:
    Sides: 4 1¼" × 19½" light fabric*; 4 1¼" × 19½" medium fabric
    Base: 1 2¼" × 19½" light fabric; 1 2¼" × 19½" medium fabric
    Zippers: 2 sturdy 19" to match light fabric
    Binding: 1" × 166" light fabric
    Straps: 2 2½" × 24" light fabric
    Interfacing: 2 2½" × 24"
*Yardage for the light fabric has been included in yardage for the pieced blocks (above)

Instructions: Select Amish Bars or Amish Central Diamond and piece 2 blocks as directed in the individual instructions.

See *Assembling a Project for Quilting* and assemble the pieced blocks as directed. For a quick project, outline-quilt each seam by machine. If hand-quilting, select some designs from those given with the templates and on page 20. Enjoy working some elaborate quilting.

Next, cut out the interior pieces from the medium fabric following the measurements given in the chart below:

INTERIOR PIECES CUTTING CHART			
Name	**Number**	**Measurements**	**Extra Supplies**
Support casing	*2*	*2" × 13"*	*2 inexpensive 12" wooden rulers*
Stencil pocket	*1*	*4" × 14"*	*½"-diameter button*
Pocket flap	*1*	*6" × 14"*	
Ruler pocket	*1*	*3" × 10½"*	
Pincushion	*1*	*3½" × 4½"*	*polyester fibrefill*
Pencil pockets	*1*	*5" × 8"*	
Book pocket	*1*	*8" × 9½"*	
Hoop holders	*4*	*1½" × 4"*	
	4	*1½" × 3½"*	*4 ½"-diameter buttons*
Thread loops	*1*	*1¼" × 12"*	*elastic—½" wide × 9"*
Thimble loops	*1*	*1¼" × 4¼"*	
Scissors pocket	*1*	*2½" × 3½"*	*polyester fibrefill*

The following instructions refer to the back or wrong side of the pieced and quilted blocks; please refer to Figure 143 during assembly. When slip-stitching the pieces in place, do not allow your stitches to go through to the other side or they will mar the pieced blocks.

Support casings: Press 1 long and 2 short edges of each strip to the wrong side; topstitch one short edge in place. Pin to the top edge of each block, centered between the sides, and with the raw edges even. Baste the raw edges together. Leaving the topstitched edge open, slip-stitch the remaining 2 edges to each block. After the project is finished, insert a 12-inch wooden ruler into each casing—not only will they provide support to the bag, but you will always have extra rulers to lend if someone else forgets theirs!

Stencil pocket: Press all raw edges ¼ inch to the wrong side; topstitch one long edge in place. Measure and mark a point 2½ inches down from the top edge of the block and 4 inches in from the left side edge; align the top left edge of the pocket with the marks. Pin to the block with the topstitched edge uppermost. Slip-stitch the sides and bottom in place. Use this pocket to store all your quilting stencils and templates. It is also a good place to keep a bar of beeswax.

Pocket flap: Fold the fabric in half lengthwise, making a 3″ × 14″ piece. Now fold in half crosswise, making a 3″ × 7″ piece. Following Figure 142, measure down one inch from the side edge and mark a dot. Using a ruler and pencil, mark a line from the bottom (fold) corner to the marked dot. Cut along this line, and discard the excess (grey area on the diagram). Open out the fabric and press. Fold in half again lengthwise with right sides facing and raw edges even. Stitch along one short edge and the long angled edge. Turn to the right side through the opening along the short unsewn edge; press. Fold the raw edge at the opening ¼ inch inside and slip-stitch in place. Make a ⅝-inch vertical buttonhole just above the point on the flap.

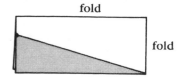

Fig. 142 Stencil pocket flap

Pin the flap to the block just above the pocket; slip-stitch the top edge in place. Sew a button to the pocket to correspond with the flap buttonhole.

Ruler pocket: Press all raw edges ¼ inch to the wrong side; topstitch one short edge in place. Measure and mark a point 1¼ inches in from the left side edge and 1¼ inches up from the bottom edge; align the bottom left side edge of the pocket with the measurement. Pin to the block with the topstitched edge uppermost. Slip-stitch the side and bottom edges in place.

Pincushion: Press all raw edges ¼ inch to the wrong side. Measure and mark a point ½ inch away from the side and flush with the top of the ruler pocket; align the top left edge of the pincushion with the measurement. Pin to the block all around. Slip-stitch in place, leaving a small opening along one side edge; stuff lightly with fibrefill through the opening, then slip-stitch the opening closed.

Pencil pockets: Press each short edge ¼ inch to the wrong side; topstitch in place. With right sides facing, fold the fabric in half crosswise, making a 5″ × 3½″ pocket; stitch along each side edge, leaving the topstitched edges open. Turn to the right side and press. Topstitch 4 or 5 narrow tubes for pencils and a seam ripper, leaving a wider tube for a rotary cutter if desired. Pin the pocket to the block ½ inch away from the ruler pocket and 1¼ inches up from the bottom. Slip-stitch the sides, bottom, and back edge of the top to the block.

Book (or magazine) pocket: Press all raw edges ¼ inch to the wrong side; topstitch one 9-inch edge in place. Pin to the block 1¼ inches up from the bottom and 1¼ inches in from the right side edge, with the topstitched edge uppermost. Slip-stitch the sides and bottom in place.

You are now finished with one side of the quilt carry-all.

Hoop holders: This Carry-All will accommodate a 14-inch-diameter round quilting hoop. For hoop holders, fold each fabric strip in half crosswise with right sides facing and raw edges even; stitch together at each long edge. Turn right side out and press. Fold the raw edges ¼ inch inside and slip-stitch each opening closed. Sew a button near one end of each 1¾-inch strip; sew a buttonhole near one end of each 2-inch strip. Place your quilting hoop in the middle of the remaining pieced block.

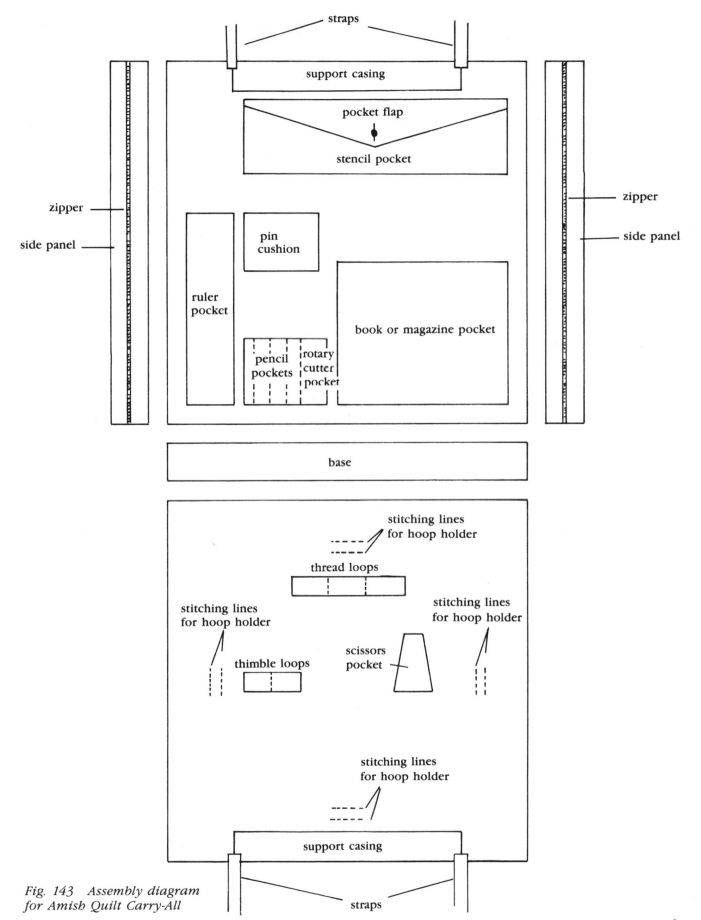

straps

support casing

pocket flap

stencil pocket

zipper

side panel

zipper

side panel

pin cushion

ruler pocket

book or magazine pocket

pencil pockets

rotary cutter pocket

base

stitching lines for hoop holder

thread loops

stitching lines for hoop holder

stitching lines for hoop holder

scissors pocket

thimble loops

stitching lines for hoop holder

support casing

straps

Fig. 143 Assembly diagram for Amish Quilt Carry-All

With a pencil, mark a short line along the inner and outer edges of the hoop at the top, bottom, and each side. Sew a buttonhole-flap along each inner marked line; sew a button-flap (with the button facing outward) along each outer marked line.

Thread loops: Fold the fabric strip in half lengthwise; stitch along one short edge and the long edge; turn right side out and press with the seam centered on one side. Fold the raw ends ¼ inch inside and slip-stitch the opening closed. Using pins, divide the fabric strip into 4 equal quarters; again using pins, divide the elastic into 4 equal quarters. Pin the elastic along the seamline of the fabric strip, matching the 4 pins only. Using the zigzag stitch on your sewing machine, sew the elastic to the fabric, pulling the elastic gently as you sew to make it fit. The fabric strip will appear slightly ruffled when finished. Pin the elastic to the block about 6 inches up from the bottom and centered between the sides, making 3 loops. Use 3 spools of quilting thread to determine the correct size of the loops. Slip-stitch in place securely at the sides and 2 middle points.

Thimble loops: Press all raw edges ¼ inch to the wrong side; topstitch in place. Pin the thimble loop to the block about 1 inch away from the right side hoop holder. Use 2 thimbles to determine the correct size of the loops. Slip-stitch in place securely at the ends and the middle.

Scissors pocket: (Adjust size if your scissors are larger). Press one short edge ¼ inch to the wrong side and topstitch in place. Position your scissors on the fabric piece; trim the sides at an angle, leaving ½ inch on each side of the blades. Press the raw edges at the sides and bottom to the wrong side. Pin to the block about 2 inches away from the left side hoop holder; slip-stitch the sides and bottom in place. Stuff the base with a small amount of fibrefill to prevent the tip of the scissors from poking through.

The interior of the Quilt Carry-All is finished.

Sides: The zipper tape (located on each side of the zipper teeth) is sandwiched by 2 strips of fabric—one light (for the outside) and one medium (for the inside). Study Figures 144 and 145 before beginning. Figure 144 shows a partial piece of fabric with the zipper beneath to demonstrate where the raw edge of the fabric should be placed for sewing. To

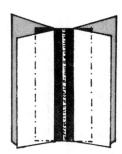

Fig. 144   Fig. 145

begin, place the right side of the light fabric on the right side of one zipper so the raw edge of the fabric overlaps the zipper teeth by about ⅜ inch. Stitch the fabric to the zipper ⅛ inch away from the zipper teeth from top to bottom, making a ¼ inch seam. Turn the zipper over. With the right side of the medium fabric facing the wrong side of the zipper, stitch in place as just described, directly over the first line of stitching. Fold both fabrics to the right side, exposing the zipper teeth, and press. Baste the raw edges together. Repeat for the other half of the zipper.

Your finished side panel should resemble Figure 145. Repeat for the other zipper.

See *Binding a Project*. Bind the top edges of the side panels on each size of the zipper teeth. At this time, also bind the top and bottom edges of each pieced block.

With the medium fabrics facing, raw edges even and the top of the zipper at the top of the block, stitch a side panel to each side edge of one pieced block. In the same manner, stitch the other edge of each side panel to the other pieced block.

Base: With wrong sides facing, baste the base pieces together around the edges. With the medium fabrics facing, stitch the base to the bottom edge of each pieced block. Stitch the short edges of the sides and the base together.

Finishing: To finish the bag, bind each of the side edges, folding the corners under neatly. Finally, bind the short raw edges between the sides and base.

For the straps, iron on or baste the interfacing to the wrong side of each fabric strip. Press each edge ¼ inch to the wrong side, then fold and press the raw edges again so they meet in the middle of the fabric strip. Topstitch each long edge in place. Fold the raw ends under, then slip-stitch to the top of the bag on the inside, on each side of each support casing.

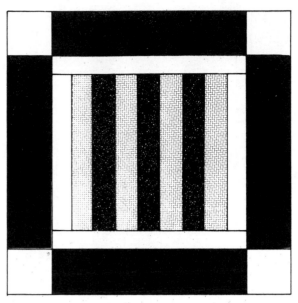

Fig. 146

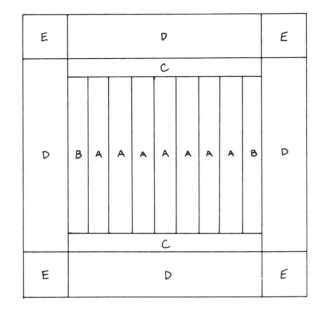

AMISH BARS

Easy
Finished size: 19" square
Pieces per block: 19

A	4 light, 3 dark	D	4 bright
B	2 medium	E	4 medium
C	2 medium		

A very traditional Amish design, Amish Bars can be made with ease and confidence by a quilter at any level of expertise.

The templates are on pages 71–73. To begin, sew each light A to a dark A, alternating colors to form the central square. Sew a B to the light A at each edge; sew a C to the top and bottom of the central square.

Sew a D to each C. Sew an E to the ends of the 2 remaining D's. Sew E-D-E to each side of the pieced block to complete the design.

Quilt a twist design on each A piece following the pattern on the template. Quilt one of the border designs in the middle of each D piece; quilt a corner design in each E piece.

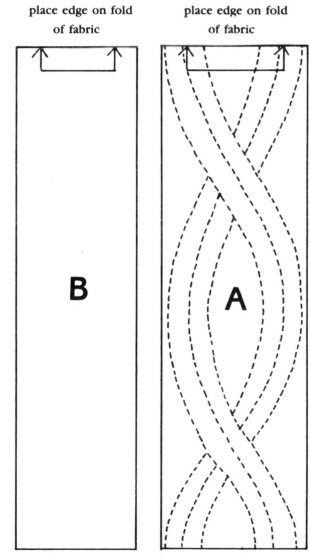

Fig. 147   Amish Bars templates

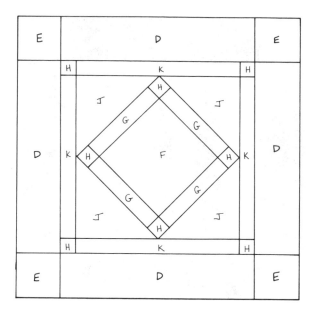

Fig. 148

AMISH CENTRAL DIAMOND

Easy
Finished size: 19" square
Pieces per block: 29

D	4 dark	H	8 bright
E	4 light	J	4 dark
F	1 bright	K	4 light
G	4 light		

Try to use traditional Amish colors to achieve a bold effect. Use solid fabrics if you want to create a feeling of Amish authenticity.

The templates are on pages 73–74. To begin, sew a G to opposite sides of F. Sew an H to each end of the remaining 2 G's, then sew H-G-H to each side of G-F-G. Sew a J to each H-G-H edge to create the central square.

Sew a K to opposite sides of the central square. Sew an H to each end of the remaining 2 K's; sew H-K-H to the top and bottom of the central square. Sew a D to each side of the central square. Sew an E to the ends of the 2 remaining D's; sew E-D-E to the top and bottom of the pieced block to complete the design.

Quilt a pinwheel in the middle of F following the pattern on the template. Quilt a palm on each J, spilling over onto each G, following the pattern on the J template. Quilt one of the border designs in the middle of each D piece; quilt a corner design in each E piece.

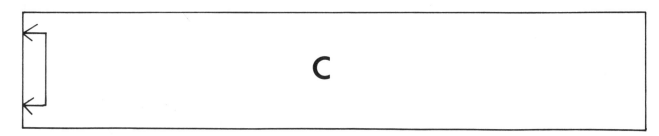

Fig. 149 Amish Bars template

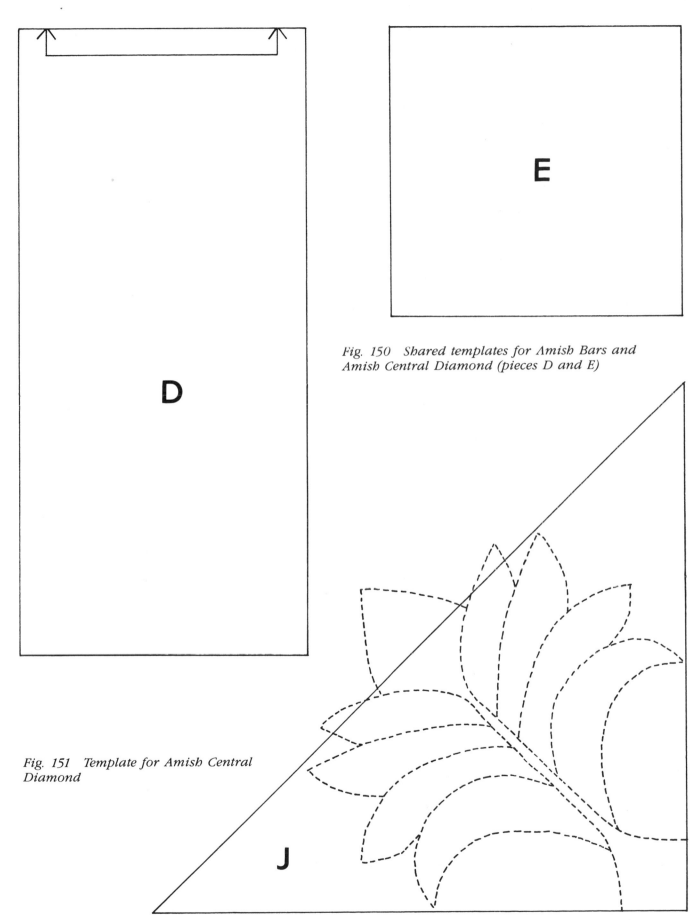

Fig. 150   Shared templates for Amish Bars and Amish Central Diamond (pieces D and E)

Fig. 151   Template for Amish Central Diamond

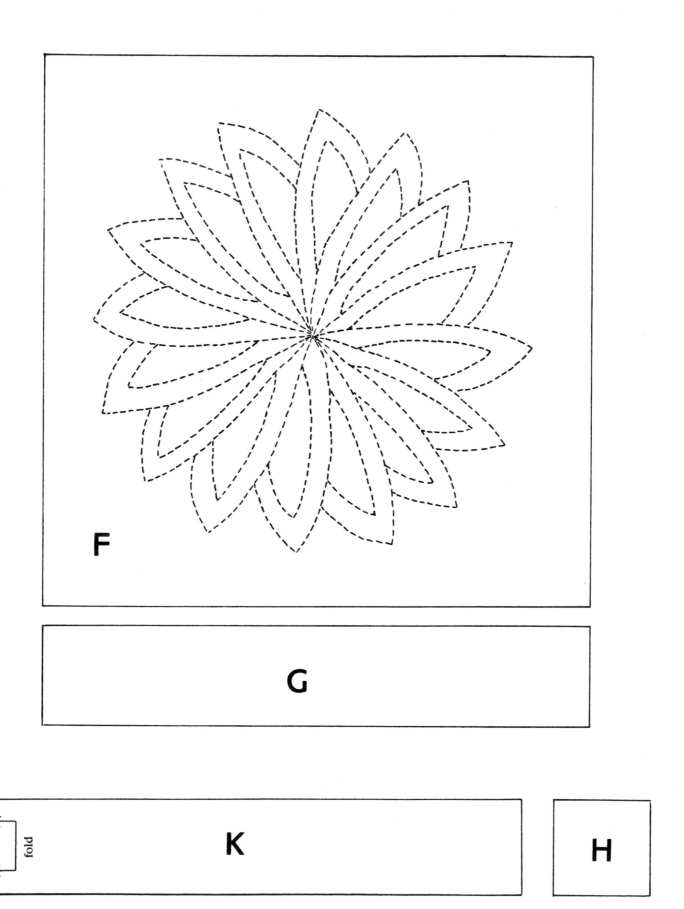

Fig. 152 Amish Central Diamond templates

74

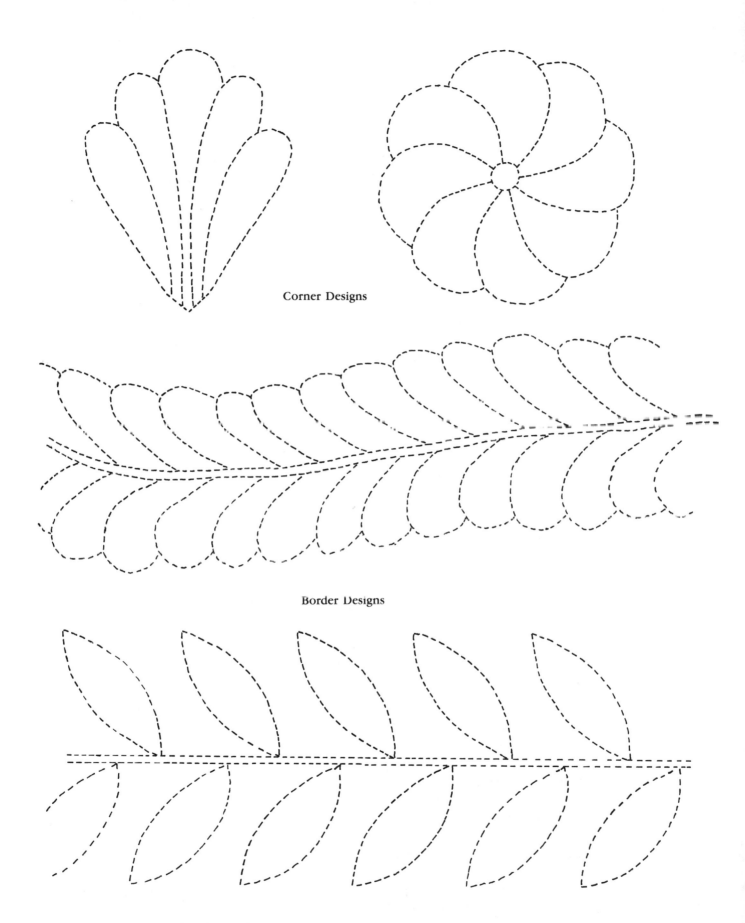

Corner Designs

Border Designs

Fig. 153   Corner and border quilting designs

FOR THE KITCHEN

Pot Holders

(Color Illus. 6 and 15A)

Fig. 154   Left to right: Small Pot Holder, Framed Pot Holder, and Round Pot Holder

Are you searching for small items to make and sell at a craft fair or bazaar? Here are 3 easy pot holders to whip up in no time flat and with a minimum of materials! Make them in bright, appealing fabrics so people will be attracted to them. Since they take very little time to make, you can price them low enough to ensure swift sales.

Use up your scraps to create cheery pot holders that will brighten up any kitchen. ¼ yard of fabric will be enough to back 7 small, 5 framed, or 4 round pot holders. Don't use fabrics that may not be flame resistant, such as fuzzy synthetics or napped fabrics. Use 2 to 3 layers of cotton or wool batting for each one to create a sturdy, usable item; do not use polyester batting. Make sure that you keep the pot holders away from naked flames. For the round pot holder (and the others too, if you wish), use purchased double-fold bias tape to save time and fabric.

Before beginning, review the following sections: *Assembling a Project for Quilting, Binding a Project,* and *Loops & Ties.*

SMALL POT HOLDER

Easy
Finished size: 6" square
Requirements
Pieced block: 1   6" square—fabric scraps
Back: 1   6½" square—fabric scrap
Batting: 2   6" square
Binding: 3   1" × 7" fabric scrap
1   1" × 9½" fabric scrap

Instructions: Select a 6-inch-square design. Piece the block following the individual instructions. Prepare the block for quilting as directed in *Assembling a Project for Quilting.* Quilt by hand or machine following the instructions given with the block.

Prepare the binding fabric and bind the sides and bottom of the pot holder; see *Binding a Project.* For the top, pin the long strip in place with the extension at the top corner; leave ¼ inch for turning at the opposite corner. Stitch as for the sides and bottom, finishing the corner. To make the loop, fold the remaining long raw edge of the extension

¼ inch to the inside to meet the central crease; fold the short end ¼ inch inside. Fold the strip in half and topstitch the long edges together. Slip-stitch the end of the extension to the back of the pot holder for the loop.

FRAMED POT HOLDER

Easy
Finished size: 8" square

Requirements

Pieced block: 1 6" square—fabric scraps
Frame: 2 1½" × 6½"; 2 1½" × 8½"—fabric scrap
Back: 1 8½" square—fabric scrap
Batting: 2 8" square
Binding: 3 1" × 9" fabric scrap
1 1" × 11½" fabric scrap

Instructions: Select a 6-inch-square design. Piece the block following the individual instructions. Sew a short frame to each side of the block; sew a long frame to the top and bottom. Prepare the block for quilting as directed in *Assembling a Project for Quilting.* Quilt by hand or machine following the instructions given with the block.

Bind the block and add the loop as directed for the Small Pot Holder.

ROUND POT HOLDER

Easy
Finished size: 9" diameter

Requirements

Pieced block: 1 6" square—fabric scraps
Border: 4 border pieces—fabric scrap
Back: 1 9½"-diameter circle—fabric scrap
Batting: 2 9"-diameter circles
Binding: 1 30" length double-fold bias tape or 1" × 30" bias strip
Loop: 1 1" × 4"—fabric scrap

Instructions: Select a 6-inch-square design. Piece the block following the individual instructions. Sew a border to each side of the block, creating a circle. Prepare the block for quilting as directed in *Assembling a Project for Quilting.* Quilt by hand or machine following the instructions given with the block.

If using a bias strip, prepare the binding; see *Binding a Project.* If using bias tape, unfold one long edge of the 30-inch strip. Pin the binding to the right side of the pot holder with raw edges even. Fold under one end and overlap with the other to conceal the raw edges. Stitch all around ¼ inch from the edges. Turn the binding over to the back and slip-stitch in place. Make the loop; see *Loops & Ties.* Slip-stitch the ends to the back of the pot holder.

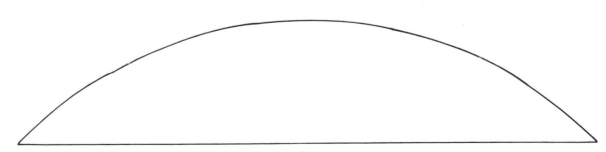

Fig. 155 Template for Round Pot Holder border

Oven Mitt

Make this useful Oven Mitt to protect your hands and arms from hot surfaces when removing dishes from the oven. It is a very simple project, easily made in just a few hours, depending on the complexity of the pieced blocks you select.

Before beginning, review the following sections: *Assembling a Project for Quilting, Machine Quilting, Binding a Project,* and *Loops & Ties.*

Easy
Finished size: 8½" × 34"
Requirements
Pieced blocks: 3   6" square—⅛ yard each of 3 to 5 fabrics
Back: 1   9" × 34½"—⅝ yard (includes fabric for remainder of project)
Batting: 1   8½" × 34"; 2   8½" × 13"
Binding: 1" × 82" bias strip (or use purchased double-fold bias tape)
Loop: 1   1" × 5"

Instructions: Select 1, 2, or 3 6-inch-square block designs; piece 3 blocks as directed in the individual instructions. Cut the following pieces from the fabric used for the back:

   4 corner triangles
   4 side triangles (place corner template on fold)
   2 ends (place template on fold)
   2 sleeves (add 6" × 8½" extension to end template)

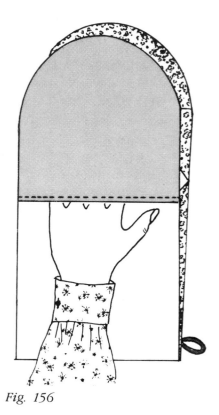

Fig. 156

Arrange the 3 pieced blocks on the diagonal as shown in the assembly diagram. Sew a corner triangle to the upper and lower left edges of block 1, and the upper and lower right edges of block 3. Sew a side triangle to the upper left and lower right edges of block 2. Then sew the remaining side

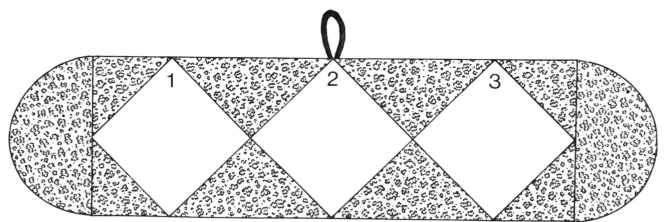

Fig. 157

triangles to the lower right edge of block 1 and the upper left edge of block 3. Join the 3 strips just made, matching seams carefully in the middle. Sew an end piece to each short edge of the pieced strip to complete the front.

Use the front as a pattern to trim away the squared edges of the back. Baste the 2 small pieces of batting to each end of the long strip of batting with raw edges even. Prepare the project for quilting as directed in *Assembling a Project for Quilting*; the 2 small pieces of batting will provide extra protection from heat at each end of the Oven Mitt. Trim the batting even with the top and back.

Hand or machine-quilt the blocks following the individual instructions. Quilt around each of the blocks, then quilt additional straight parallel lines every ⅜ inch to echo the edges of the blocks.

Press the straight edge of each sleeve ¼ inch to the wrong side twice; topstitch in place. With the wrong side of the sleeve facing the back of the project and raw edges even, stitch each sleeve in place, about ⅛ inch from the edges, leaving the top-stitched edge open.

If using a bias strip, prepare the binding; see *Binding a Project*. If using bias tape, unfold one long edge of the strip. Pin the binding to the right side of the oven glove with raw edges even. Fold under one end and overlap with the other to conceal the raw edges. Stitch all around ¼ inch from the edges. Turn the binding over to the back and slip-stitch in place. Make the loop; see *Loops & Ties*. Slip-stitch the ends to the back of the Oven Mitt just above the middle block.

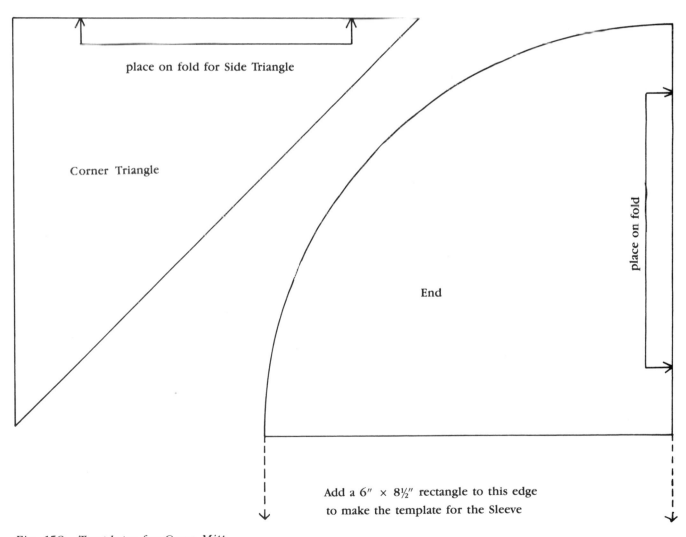

place on fold for Side Triangle

Corner Triangle

End

place on fold

Add a 6″ × 8½″ rectangle to this edge
to make the template for the Sleeve

Fig. 158   Templates for Oven Mitt

Patchwork Apron

(Color Illus. 6)

Make this charming Patchwork Apron to wear in the kitchen—it's perfect for picnics and outdoor parties too! You'll feel so good with it on, that you may not want to take it off when your work is finished!

Be sure to pre-wash all your fabrics carefully before beginning so that your apron can be laundered easily without your worrying about bleeding fabrics or shrinkage.

Moderate
Size: Small (4–6), medium (8–10) and large (12–14). The apron is designed to be worn quite long; if you prefer a shorter apron, adjust the length of the skirt accordingly.

Requirements
Pieced block: 1 6" square—fabric scraps
Fabric (45" wide): ⅞ yard (small); 1¼ yards (medium); 1⅜ yards (large) of plain cotton or cotton-blend fabric such as muslin. For Border around Pieced Block and Seminole Patchwork Band: ⅛ yard print, ⅛ yard bright, ⅛ yard medium (small); ¼ yard print, ⅛ yard bright, ⅛ yard
medium (medium); ¼ yard print, ⅛ yard bright, ⅛ yard medium (large). Print fabric should coordinate with the plain fabric.
Interfacing: ⅛ yard
Buttons: 2 ½" diameter

Instructions: Select a 6-inch-square design. Piece the block following the individual instructions. Cut the pieces for the apron following the measurements given in the chart below; all measurements include a ¼" seam allowance.

For the medium and large sizes, sew a short print border to the top and bottom of the pieced block. Sew a long border to each side of the block. With right sides facing and raw edges even, stitch the bib to the bib back along the top edge only. Turn to the right side and press. Baste the raw edges together at the sides and bottom.

For the straps, press each fabric strip in half lengthwise with wrong sides facing. Press one long edge of each strap ¼ inch to the wrong side. With right sides facing and raw edges even, stitch a strap to each side of the bib so the raw edges are flush

CUTTING CHART FOR APRON			
Piece	**Small**	**Medium**	**Large**
Bib borders (print)	none	2: 1½" × 6½" 2: 1½" × 8½"	2: 2½" × 6½" 2: 2½" × 10½"
Bib back (plain)	1: 6½" × 6½"	1: 8½" × 8½"	1: 10½" × 10½"
Straps (plain)	2: 2" × 20"	2: 2½" × 36"	2: 3" × 40"
Waistband (plain) Interfacing	2: 2" × 20" 1: 2" × 20"	2: 2½" × 27" 1: 2½" × 27"	2: 2½" × 32" 1: 2½" × 32"
Ties (plain)	2: 3" × 16"	2: 4" × 20"	2: 4" × 24"
Skirt (plain)	1: 19" × 29"	1: 24" × 40"	1: 26" × 45"
Seminole patchwork band (optional): Print Bright Medium	1: 1" × 44" 1: 1¼" × 44" 1: 1¼" × 44"	1: 1" × 60" 1: 1¼" × 60" 1: 1¼" × 60"	1: 1" × 72" 1: 1¼" × 72" 1: 1¼" × 72"
Band borders (print)	2: ¾" × 29"	2: ¾" × 40"	2: ¾" × 45"
Band facing	1: 2" × 29"	1: 2" × 40"	1: 2" × 45"

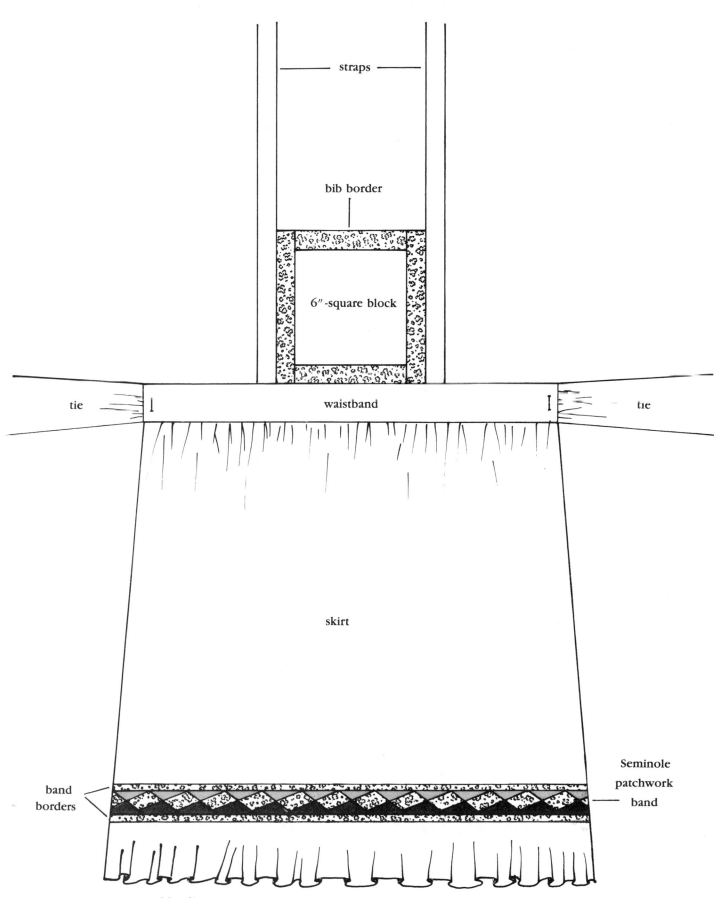

Fig. 159   Apron assembly diagram

at the bottom. Press the seam allowance towards the strap. Continue pressing the raw edge of the strap above the bib ¼ inch to the wrong side. Pin the long pressed edges of the strap together, sandwiching the raw edges inside; on the bib, pin the strap over the seam allowance. Topstitch the pressed edges in place, then topstitch along the opposite long edge of each strap.

Sew or iron on the interfacing to the waistband. Find the crosswise middle of that waistband and the bottom of the bib; mark each point with a pin. With right sides facing, raw edges even and pins matching, pin the bib strap piece to the waistband; stitch together.

For the ties, trim off one end of each at a 45 degree angle. Press the angled edge and both long edges ¼ inch to the wrong side twice, enclosing the raw edges. Topstitch in place. Baste ¼ inch from the raw edge on each end. Gather the basted edge to fit the ends of the waistband. Pin, then stitch each tie to the waistband, with right sides facing and raw edges even. Press the seam allowances towards the waistband.

Press one long edge of the remaining waistband piece (the facing) ¼ inch to the wrong side. Pin the facing to the waistband with right sides together, raw edges even and the bib and ties sandwiched in between. Stitch across the short ends and the long edge, angling your stitching sharply at each corner. Trim off the seam allowances at the corners; turn to the right side and press. Set aside.

To add the Seminole patchwork band to the skirt, measure and mark a line 3½ inches above and parallel to one long edge of the skirt fabric. Cut along the line.

To make the pieced band, sew the bright and medium fabric strips to opposite sides of the print fabric strip. Your pieced strip will resemble Figure 160. Next, using a ruler, measure and mark off

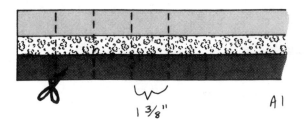

Fig. 160

82

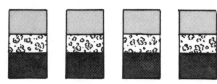

Fig. 161

1⅜-inch wide pieces across the entire strip; cut along each marked line. Your pieces should be arranged following Figure 161. Sew the strips together matching the seams indicated by the arrows in Figure 162. Your pieced strip should look like

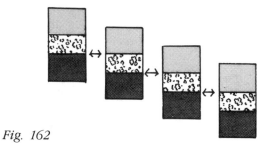

Fig. 162

Figure 163. Using a ruler and pencil, draw a straight line across the top and bottom to eliminate the staggered edges; make sure the width of the piece you have marked is 1½ inches. Trim off the excess

Fig. 163

fabric along the marked lines. Press gently because the strip is now on the bias and will tend to stretch. Sew two band border strips to opposite sides of the pieced band; you may need to trim off a bit of the pieced band to align the ends.

Stitch the Seminole patchwork band between the cut edges of the apron skirt. Press the seam allowances towards the band. Press the long edges of the band facing ¼ inch to the wrong side. Pin the facing over the wrong side of the band and slipstitch in place, covering all raw edges.

Fold and press the bottom and 2 side edges of the skirt ¼ inch to the wrong side twice, enclosing all raw edges. Topstitch in place. Machine-baste 2 lines of stitching, ⅛ and ¼ inch away from the raw top edge. Gently pull the basting threads to gather the top edge of the skirt to fit the bottom of the waistband. With right sides facing, raw edges even and keeping the waistband facing out of the way, pin the skirt to the waistband, adjusting gathers evenly. Stitch in place; press the seam allowance towards the waistband. Slip-stitch the pressed bottom edge of the waistband facing over the seam allowance, hiding all raw edges.

Make a vertical buttonhole, ⅝ inch long, at each end of the waistband. Try on the apron, tying the ties comfortably behind you. Pin the end of the shoulder straps to the end of the waistband, just behind the buttonholes so that the straps criss-cross over your back. Take off the apron. You may find that you need to trim off some of the strap; do so, leaving a ¼-inch seam allowance. Fold the seam allowance ⅛ inch to the wrong side twice and topstitch in place. Mark the position for each button on the straps, then sew a button in place on each.

Tray Cloth

(Color Illus. 15B)

Fig. 164

Fig. 165

Brighten up your morning breakfast tray with a lively Tray Cloth. It can be whipped up in a very short time and will look equally well gracing a bureau or sideboard.

Easy
Finished size: 8″ × 15″
Requirements
Pieced blocks: 2 6″ square—fabric scraps
Inner border: 2 1½″ × 6½″—⅛ yard dark fabric
2 1½″ × 14½″
Outer border: 2 1″ × 14½″—⅛ yard bright fabric
2 1″ × 8½″
Back: 1 8½″ × 15½″—¼ yard light fabric

Instructions: Select a 6-inch-square design. Piece 2 blocks following the individual instructions. Sew the 2 blocks together, matching seams carefully.

Sew a short inner border to each side of the blocks. Sew a long inner border to the top and bottom. Sew the long outer borders to the top and bottom; then sew the remaining border strips to each side.

With right sides facing and raw edges even, stitch the pieced front to the back all around, leaving a 3″ opening for turning along one edge. Clip away the seam allowances at the corners; then turn right side out, carefully poking out the corners. Fold the raw edges at the opening ¼ inch inside, then slip-stitch the opening closed. Press carefully.

Topstitch along the edges of each border, then topstitch the blocks, following the individual instructions for quilting.

Kitchen Set

Fig. 166

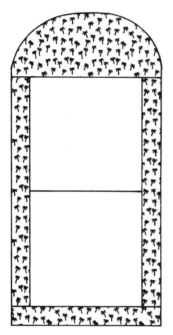

Fig. 167   Blender Cover

Disguise your kitchen equipment when not in use with these attractive patchwork covers. They take no time to make and will enhance the appearance of your kitchen work area considerably.

The toaster cover is designed to fit a standard 2-slice toaster; instructions for a 4-slice toaster cover are included. If you are covering a toaster oven, enlarge the central strip to the depth of your toaster oven and adjust the size of the side pieces as necessary. The blender cover will fit any standard-size blender.

Choose from one of 3 edge finishes: plain (not shown), ruffled (shown on the toaster cover), or piped (shown on the blender cover).

Before beginning, review the following sections: *Assembling a Project for Quilting, Machine Quilting, Binding a Project, Ruffles, Piping.*

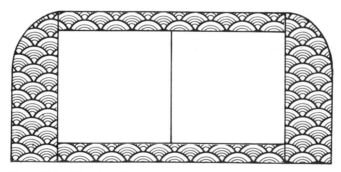

Fig. 168   Toaster Cover

TOASTER COVER (2 SLICE)

Easy

Size: About 11" wide × 8" high × 5" deep

Requirements

Pieced block: 1 6" square—scraps or ⅛ yard each of 3 to 5 fabrics

Remainder of project: ¼ yard

Top/Bottom strips: 2 1½" × 6½"

Sides: 2 (using template)

Central strip: 1 5½" × 25"

Lining: ¼ yard

Batting: 2 8½" × 11½"

1 5½" × 25"

Binding: 2 1¼" × 11½"—¼ yard (includes fabric for ruffle or piping)

2 1¼" × 5½"

Trim (optional): Ruffle: 1 1½" × 66"

***OR** Piping: 1 1" × 26"*

Instructions: Select a 6-inch-square block design. Piece the appropriate number of blocks for the 2- or 4-slice toaster cover as directed in the individual requirements lists. If making the 4-slice toaster, stitch the blocks together, matching seams carefully.

Sew the top and bottom strips to opposite edges of the block(s). Sew a side to each remaining edge, matching the dots to the seams. Press carefully.

•Use the pieced front as a pattern to cut one back (from matching fabric), 2 linings, and 2 pieces of batting. Use the central strip as a pattern to cut one lining.

Assemble the front, back, and central strip for quilting as directed in *Assembling a Project for Quilting,* using the linings as the back of each piece. Machine-quilt the block(s) following the individual instructions. Stitch close to the raw edges of the front, back, and central strip, securing the 3 layers of each together.

Bind each of the straight bottom edges of the front and back and the short edges of the central strip as directed in *Binding a Project.* Skip the next paragraph if you are using a plain finish.

If adding a ruffle or piping, review the instructions on making and attaching a ruffle or piping. Attach the ruffle or piping to the curved edge of the front (it will overlap the binding at each bottom edge) the ends of the ruffle or piping should be finished neatly and should be flush with the bottom edge of the front.

With right sides facing, raw edges even and bound edges flush, pin the front to the central strip, sandwiching the ruffle or piping in between (if using either of these); ease the pieces carefully together around the curves. Stitch together, backstitching at each end. Trim the seam, then zigzag-stitch the raw edges together.

Add the back to the central strip in the same manner to complete the cover.

TOASTER COVER (4 SLICE)

Easy

Size: About 17" wide × 8" high × 5½" deep

Requirements

Pieced blocks: 2 6" square—scraps or ⅛ yard each of 3 to 5 fabrics

Remainder of project: ½ yard

Top/Bottom strips: 2 1½" × 12½"

Sides: 2 (using template)

Central strip: 6" × 28½"

Lining: ½ yard

Batting: 2 8½" × 17½"

1 6" × 28½"

Binding: 2 1¼" × 17½"—¼ yard (includes fabric for ruffle or piping)

2 1¼" × 6½"

Trim (optional): Ruffle: 1 1½" × 72"

***OR** Piping: 1 1" × 29"*

Instructions: See 2-slice Toaster Cover.

BLENDER COVER

Size: About 16¼" high × 8" wide × 8" deep

Requirements

Pieced blocks: 2 6" square—scraps or ⅛ yard each of 3 to 5 fabrics

Remainder of Project: ½ yard

Top: 1 (using template)

Bottom: 1 1½" × 8½"

Sides: 2 1½" × 12½"

Central strip: 1 8½" × 37½"

Lining: ½ yard

Batting: 2 8½" × 16¾"

1 8½" × 37½"

Binding: 4 1¼" × 8½"—¼ yard (includes fabric for ruffle or piping)

Trim: (optional): Ruffle: 1 1½" × 91"

***OR** Piping: 1 1" × 38"*

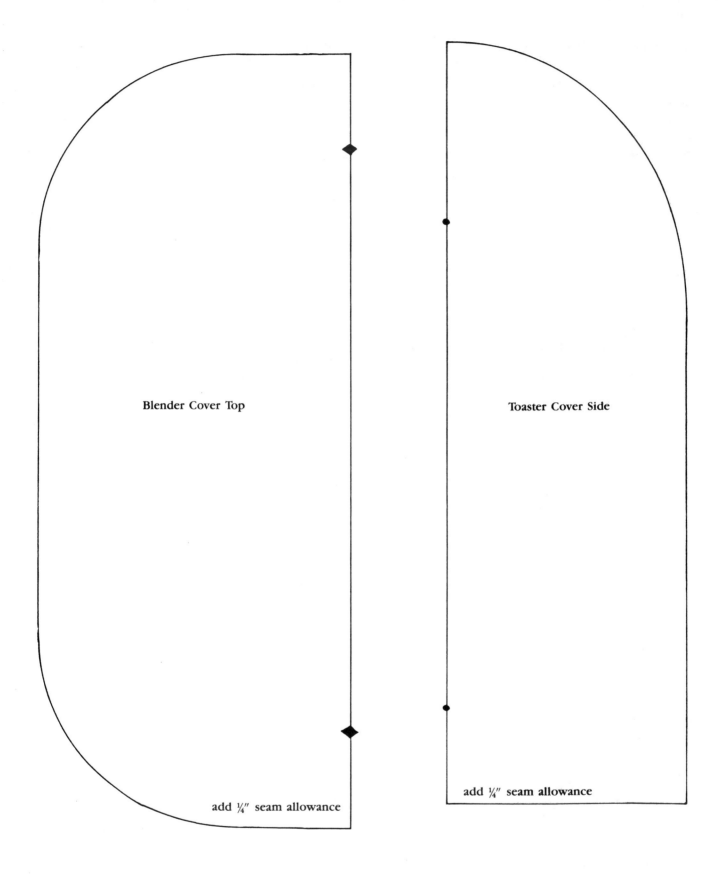

Blender Cover Top

Toaster Cover Side

add ¼″ seam allowance

add ¼″ seam allowance

Fig. 169   Template for Blender Cover top (left) and Toaster Cover side piece (right)

Instructions: Select a 6-inch-square block design. Piece 2 blocks following the individual instructions. Sew the blocks together, matching seams carefully.

Stitch a side to each long edge of the pieced blocks; sew the top to the top edge, matching the notches to the seams. Sew the bottom to the remaining edge. Press carefully.

Complete the Blender Cover by following the instructions for the Toaster Cover, starting at the •.

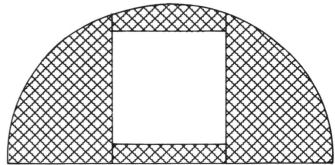

Fig. 170   Tea Cozy

TEA COZY

Keep your pot of tea warm by covering it with this Tea Cozy. Make it as a gift for a special tea-lover in your life. The Cozy will fit most teapots. To make it smaller, simply trim a bit away from the side pieces.

Before beginning, review the following sections: *Assembling a Project for Quilting, Machine Quilting,* and *Binding a Project.*

Easy
Size: About 16½" wide × 8" high
Requirements
Pieced block: 1   6" square—scraps or ⅛ yard each of 3 to 5 fabrics
Remainder of Project: ¼ yard
*   Top: 1 (using template)*
*   Bottom: 1   1½" × 6½"*
*   Sides: 2 (using template)*
Lining: ¼ yard
Batting: 2   8½" × 17"
Binding: 2   1¼" × 17½"—⅛ yard
*   1   1¼" × 27"*

Instructions: Select one of the 6-inch-square block designs. Piece as directed in the individual instructions.

Sew the top piece to the top edge of the block; sew the bottom to the opposite edge. Sew a side to each remaining edge. Press carefully.

Use the pieced front as a pattern to cut one back (from matching fabric), 2 linings, and 2 pieces of batting.

Assemble the front and back for quilting as directed in *Assembling a Project for Quilting,* using the linings as the back of each piece. Machine-quilt the block following the individual instructions. Stitch close to the raw edges of the front and back, securing the 3 layers together.

Bind the straight bottom edges of the front and back as directed in *Binding a Project.* Baste the front and back together around the curved edges with lining sides facing. Bind the curved edges of the Tea Cozy, turning the ends under neatly to finish.

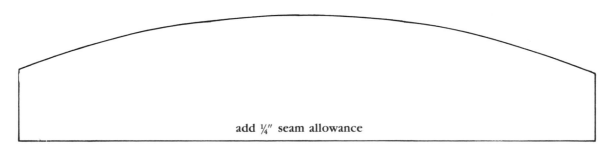

add ¼" seam allowance

Fig. 171   Template for top of Tea Cozy

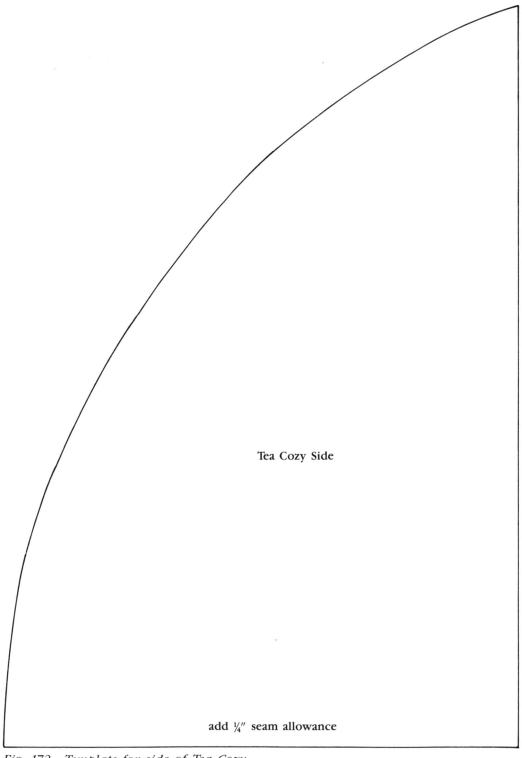

Tea Cozy Side

add ¼″ seam allowance

Fig. 172   Template for side of Tea Cozy

Table Centerpiece

(Color Illus. 14B)

Fig. 173

If you have a lovely wooden table, why hide it beneath a tablecloth? Instead, make this unusual centerpiece to enhance your beautiful wood. It is very simple to make, and would work just as well on a bureau or side table.

You'll find that the 6-inch-square block designs offer many possibilities when combined in groups of 4. Literally hundreds of designs can be made by turning the designs in different directions. Make a small tracing of the blocks you like, to see what they'll look like when sewn together in fours. If you're like me, you'll have a hard time choosing which one to make first!

Coordinate the fabrics in your blocks with those used for the border of the centerpiece to create a cohesive design. The block design shown in the photograph is a tricky one, but the results are spectacular.

Easy
Size: 14"-wide octagon
Requirements
Pieced blocks: 4   6" square (yardage listed below)
Back: 1   16" square light fabric
Batting: 14½" square
Binding: self-binding
Fabric: light—½ yard; bright—¼ yard; medium I—¼ yard; medium II—¼ yard; dark—⅛ yard (or use scraps for the ⅛ and ¼ yardages)

Instructions: Select a 6-inch-square design. Piece 4 blocks as directed in the individual instructions. Arrange the squares in a block, turning the designs to get the best possible effect. When satisfied with your arrangement, sew 2 pairs of squares together for each half, then sew the halves together, matching seams carefully, to complete the middle of the centerpiece. Cut the following pieces using the templates:

A	8 medium I, 8 medium II, 8 dark	D	4 light, 4 light reversed
B	24 light, 24 light reversed	E	4 medium II
C	4 dark	F	4 bright, 4 bright reversed

Make 24 A-B squares by sewing a B to each angled edge of A. Make 4 C-D squares by sewing a D to each angled edge of C. Arrange the squares around the pieced middle as shown in the assembly diagram, or in whichever arrangement you wish—you may find that by turning the squares in different ways you can create an effect more compatible with the design you have chosen.

Sew the A-B squares together making 4 strips with 6 squares in each strip. Sew an A-B strip to each side of the middle. Sew a C-D square to each end of the 2 remaining strips; sew to the top and bottom of the middle.

Sew an F to each side of each E. Sew F-E-F to each edge of the middle to complete the pieced top.

See *Assembling a Project for Quilting*; assemble the project as directed. Trim the corners from the batting even with the top; trim the corners from the back, allowing a 1-inch margin at each edge. Quilt each of the blocks by hand or machine following the individual instructions. Outline-quilt each A, C and E piece, then quilt parallel lines across each F piece as shown in the assembly diagram.

See *Binding a Project*; self-bind all edges of the centerpiece as directed, mitring each of the corners; see *How to Mitre Corners*.

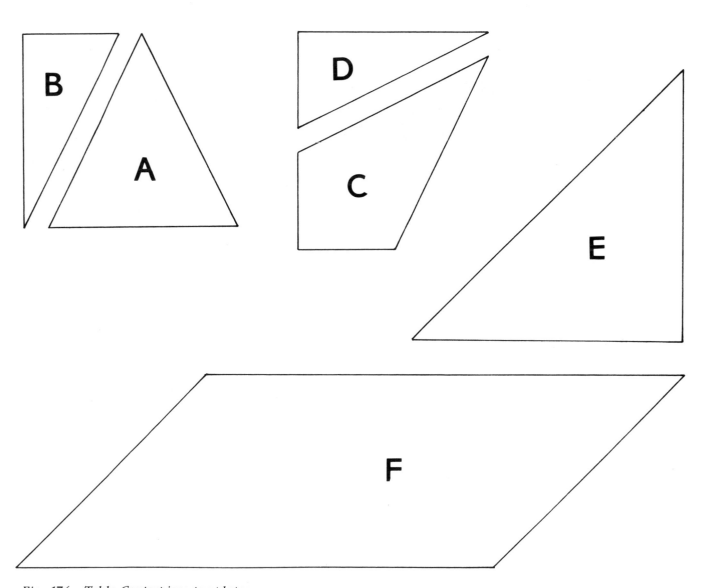

Fig. 174   *Table Centerpiece templates*

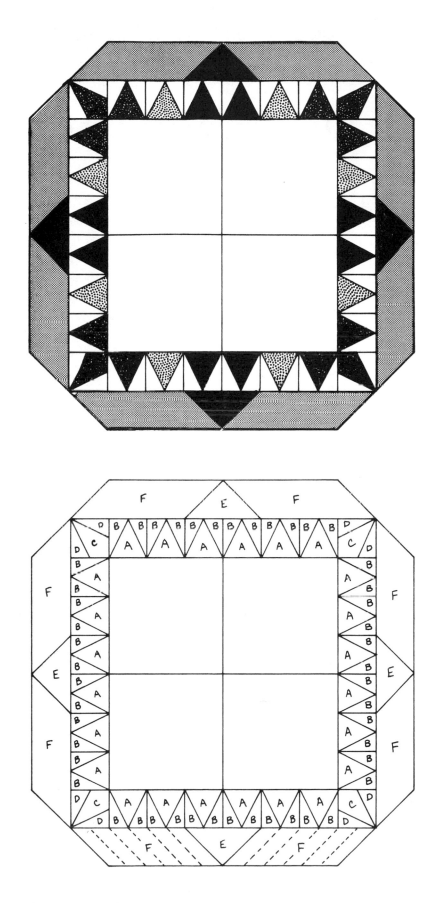

Fig. 175   Table Centerpiece assembly diagrams

FOR THE HOME

Quick Patchwork Pillows

(Color Illus. 4A, 4B, 5A and 5B)

Question: What adds color, coziness, and comfort to any room in the house? Answer: A patchwork pillow. Simple, fast and inexpensive to make, pillows are high on my list of favorite projects. The 4 pillow styles given here have been designed to appeal to a variety of tastes.

General Instructions: Select one of the following pillow designs and a 6-inch-square block design. Piece the required number of blocks as directed in the individual instructions.

Follow the requirements and individual instructions for assembling your chosen pillow style. If you wish to quilt the top before making your pillow, cut a piece of muslin (or any neutral fabric) the same size as your top for the back; cut a piece of batting to the same size. See *Assembling a Project for Quilting*; quilt the pillow top following the individual instructions for the blocks, and your own design for the sides or borders (if any).

See *Ruffle, Lace,* or *Piping* for instructions on making and attaching a ruffle or piping. After the ruffles, lace, or piping have been added, prepare the back in one of the following methods.

Zipper opening: Cut the fabric to the required size; with right sides facing, machine-baste the long edges together, making a ½-inch seam. (If the zipper is shorter than the length of the seam, mark off the zipper length, centered evenly between top and bottom; stitch the seam with small stitches above and below the zipper markings.) Press the seam open. Sew the zipper in place following the manufacturer's instructions (Fig. 176).

Flap opening: Cut the fabric to the required length. Press one long edge of each piece ¼ inch to the wrong side twice to conceal raw edges; stitch in place for a finished edge. Lap the finished edge of the smaller piece 2 inches over the larger one; baste in place at the top and bottom (Fig. 177).

When the back has been prepared, pin to the front with right sides together, raw edges even and any ruffles, lace, or piping sandwiched between them. Stitch together ¼ inch from the edges all around. Clip off each of the 4 corners at an angle (Fig. 178), unless the pillow is oval, then turn to the right side. Insert the pillow form through the zipper or flap opening in the back.

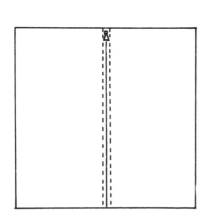

Fig. 176

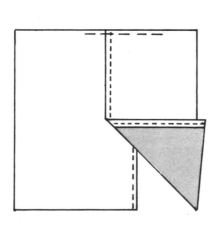

Fig. 177

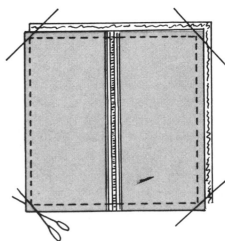

Fig. 178

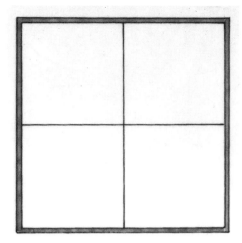

Fig. 179 Square Pillow

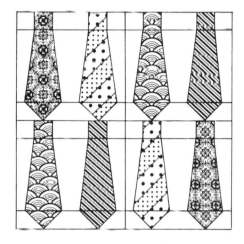

Fig. 180 Square Pillow with Dad's Ties design

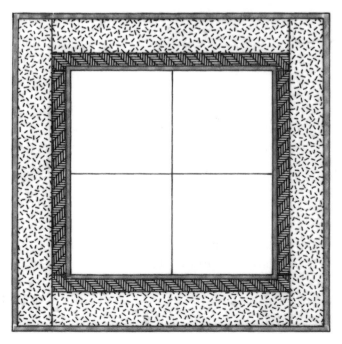

Fig. 181 Square Pillow with Borders & Piping

SQUARE PILLOW

Easy
Finished size: 12" square

Requirements

Pieced blocks: 4 6" square—fabric scraps
Piping cord: ¼" diameter—1⅜ yards
Piping fabric: 1 2" × 50"—fabric scrap or ⅛ yard
Back (choose one method): ⅜ yard
   Zipper opening: 2 6¾" × 12½"
   Flap opening: 1 6½" × 12½"
              1 8½" × 12½"
Zipper (optional): 1 12" long
Pillow form: 1 12" square

Join the 4 pieced blocks to form the pillow front. Stitch the piping to the pillow front all around before attaching the back.

SQUARE PILLOW WITH BORDERS & PIPING

Easy
Finished size: 18" square

Requirements

Pieced blocks: 4 6" square—fabric scraps
Piping cord: ¼" diameter—3½ yards
Dark piping fabric: 1 2" × 50"—¼ yard
                     1 2" × 75"
Medium border fabric: 2 1½" × 12½"—⅛ yard
                     2 1½" × 14½"
Bright border fabric: 2 2½" × 14½"—¼ yard
                     2 2½" × 18½"
Back (choose one method): ½ yard
   Zipper opening: 2 9¾" × 18½"
   Flap opening: 1 9½" × 18½"
              1 11½" × 18½"
Zipper (optional): 1 18" long
Pillow form: 18" square

Join the 4 pieced blocks to form a square (the middle). Make 2 separate lengths of piping. Sew the shorter piping to the pieced middle all around, angling the piping sharply at each corner. Sew a short medium border strip to each side edge of the block with the piping sandwiched in between. Sew a long medium border strip to the top and bottom of the block, again sandwiching the piping in between. Sew a short bright border strip to the top and bottom of the block; sew a long bright border strip to each side of the block. Stitch the remaining length of piping to the pillow front all around before attaching the back.

Fig. 182 Square Ruffled Pillow

Fig. 183 Oval Ruffled Pillow

SQUARE RUFFLED PILLOW

Easy

Finished size (excluding ruffle): 17" square

Requirements

Pieced blocks: 4 6" square—fabric scraps

Right-angle triangles: 4 9" × 9" × 12½"—⅜ yard

Fabric for ruffle: 3½" × 140"—⅜ yard

Back (choose one method): ½ yard
  Zipper opening: 2 9¼" × 17½"
  Flap opening: 1 9" × 17½"
  *   1 11" × 17½"*

Zipper (optional): 1 16" long

Pillow form: 2 17½" squares of muslin—½ yard

Polyester fibrefill

Join the 4 pieced blocks to form a square (the middle). Sew a right-angle triangle to each edge of the pieced middle. Stitch the ruffle to the pillow front all around before attaching the back.

To make the pillow form, sew the muslin squares together making a ¼-inch seam and leaving a 3-inch opening along one edge. Turn right side out. Stuff firmly with fibrefill, fold the raw edges at the opening inside and slip-stitch closed.

OVAL RUFFLED PILLOW

Easy

Finished size (excluding ruffle): About 12" × 14"

Requirements

Pieced blocks: 2 6" square—fabric scraps

Border fabric: ¼ yard

Fabric for ruffle: 1 3" × 96"—¼ yard

Back (choose one method): ½ yard
  Zipper opening: 2 8" × 12½"
  Flap opening: 1 8" × 12½"
  *   1 10" × 12½"*

Zipper (optional): 1 12" long

Pillow form: 2 12½" × 14½" muslin rectangles—⅜ yard

Polyester fibrefill

Use the templates to cut 2 side pieces and 2 top/bottom pieces. Sew the pieced blocks together, matching seams carefully to form a rectangle (the middle). Sew the top and bottom pieces to the middle, then sew the sides in place, creating an oval shape. Prepare the back as directed, then center the pillow front over the back and the 2 muslin rectangles; trim away the excess fabric even with the edges of the pillow front. Stitch the ruffle to the pillow front all around, then stitch the back in place.

To make the pillow form, sew the muslin ovals together making a ¼-inch seam and leaving a 3-inch opening along one edge. Turn right side out. Stuff firmly with fibrefill, fold the raw edges at the opening inside and slip-stitch closed.

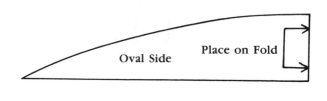

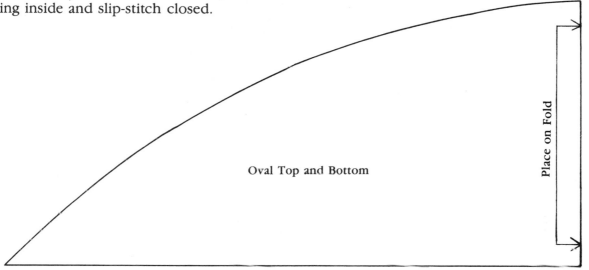

Fig. 184 Templates for Oval Pillow

95

Letter Holder

Organize your letters and bills by storing them in this attractive wall hanging. There is a choice of 2 different styles—the one shown in the photograph (A) would fit in any decor, while the other one pictured (B) would be perfect in a child's room (for storing small toys or clothes). Both are very quick and easy projects.

Before beginning, review the following sections: *Binding a Project, Piping, Assembling a Project for Quilting, Machine Quilting,* and *Hanging a Patchwork Project.*

Easy
Size: (A) 10" × 28"; (B) 10" × 30"

Requirements
Pieced blocks: 3   6" square—⅛ yard each of 3 to 5 fabrics
Batting: 3   6" square
Back of blocks (for quilting): 3   6½" square—¼ yard muslin
Remainder of hanging: (A) ⅝ yard; (B) ⅝ yard plus 76 border squares, each 1½" × 1½" cut from fabric scraps
Binding for blocks: 3   1½" × 6½"
Central panel: 1   6½" × 28½"
Side panels: (A) 2   2½" × 28½"; (B) 2   1½" × 28½"
Back: (A) 10½" × 28½"; (B) 10½" × 30½"
For hanging: 2" × 28" sleeve
Piping: (A) ¼" diameter—1⅝ yards
Piping fabric: (A) 2   1" × 29"—fabric scrap
Batting: (A) 10" × 28"; (B) 10" × 30"
Binding (optional): (A) 2   1½" × 10½", 2   1½" × 29"; (B) 2   1" × 10½", 2   1" × 31"

Instructions: Select three 6-inch-square designs. Piece each block following the individual instructions. Baste a square of batting to the back of each pieced block so there is a ¼-inch allowance of fabric around all edges of the batting. Pin a muslin back to each block with right sides facing and raw edges even. Stitch together along the bottom edge of each block. Fold to the right side, sandwiching the batting in between, and press the stitched edge very lightly (so as not to affect the batting); baste the remaining raw edges together. Bind the top edge of each block as directed in *Binding a Project.*

Fig. 185

Using a pencil and ruler, measure and mark 3 lines across the central panel, the following distances down from the short (top) edge: 2½ inches, 11½ inches, and 20½ inches. Position the 3 pieced blocks on the central panel so the top bound edges of the blocks match the marked lines and pin in place. Baste the side edges of the blocks to the panel; slip-stitch the base of each block to the panel.

For A (this step is optional for B), cut 2 lengths of piping cord, each 29 inches. Review *Piping* for instructions on making and attaching the piping,

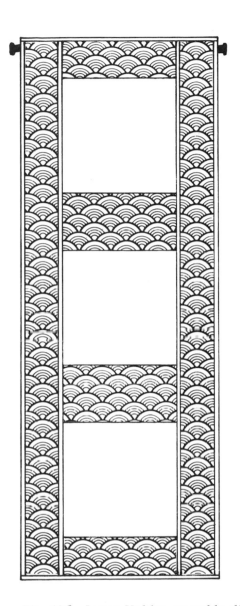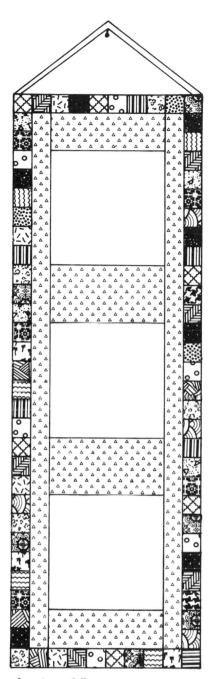

Fig. 186 *Letter Holder assembly diagrams for A and B*

then attach the piping to each side of the central panel.

Next, sew a side panel to each long edge of the central panel, sandwiching the edges of the blocks (and piping, if used) in between.

For B, sew the 76 squares into 4 strips, making 2 strips of 28 squares and 2 strips of 10 squares. Sew the long strips to each side of the project; sew the short strips to the top and bottom.

See *Assembling a Project for Quilting* and assemble the hanging as directed. Machine-quilt

along the seam between the central and side panels; for B, also machine-quilt between the side panels and the pieced border.

Bind the edges of the project or fold the raw edges of the front and back ¼ inch inside and slip-stitch together.

See *Hanging a Patchwork Project*; make and attach a sleeve or strap as directed.

Table Runner

Fig. 187

A patchwork runner can add sparkle to your table—use it on a plain surface, or place the runner on top of a tablecloth. This design can also be used to decorate a sideboard or bureau, and it can even hang on the wall to fill a narrow space!

Easy
Finished size: 8" × 26"
Requirements
Pieced blocks: 4   6" square—¼ yard each of 3 to 5 fabrics
Border: 2   1½" × 6½" —⅛ yard
*   2   1½" × 24½"*
*   4   1½" squares—fabric scrap*
Back: 1   8½" × 26½" —¼ yard

Instructions: Select a 6-inch-square design. Piece 4 blocks following the individual instructions. Sew the blocks together, matching seams carefully, to make a long strip.

Sew a long border to the top and bottom edges of the strip. Sew a square to each end of the remaining 2 border pieces, then sew the borders to each end of the long strip.

With right sides facing and raw edges even, stitch the pieced front to the back all around, leaving a 3-inch opening for turning along one edge. Clip away the seam allowances at the corners, then turn right side out. Fold the raw edges at the opening ¼ inch inside; slip-stitch the opening closed. Press carefully.

Topstitch along the outer edges of the project, then along the inner edges of the border. Topstitch the blocks, following the individual instructions for quilting.

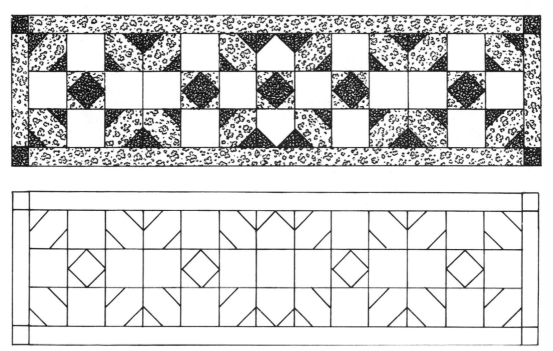

Fig. 188   *Table Runner Variation made with Coming of Spring blocks*

Table Runner Variations: Sometimes adding an extra pieced strip between the central blocks will create an unusual effect. Play around with the design to see if you can come up with your own variations. If you do add some pieces, measure your finished pieced strip and adjust the length of the long borders accordingly. The back must be adjusted by the same width.

Fig. 189   *Table Runner Variation made with Devil's Advocate blocks*

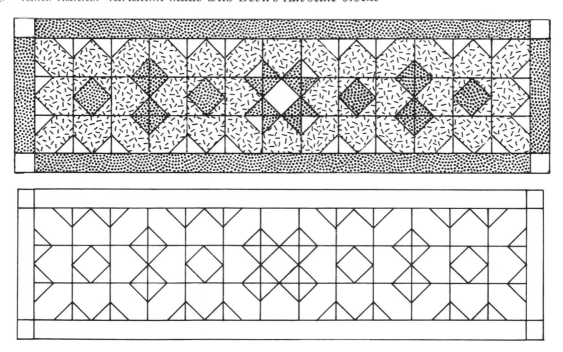

Treasure Box

Fig. 190

Store your favorite pieces of jewelry or cherished mementoes in this softly padded Treasure Box. Practical yet pretty as a picture, it can be made in fabrics to match your color scheme, or in bright materials to accent a college dorm room or other small place.

Moderate
Finished size: 6" × 12" × 3" high
Requirements
Pieced blocks: 2   6" square—fabric scraps or ⅛ yard each of 3 to 5 fabrics
Matching fabric: ½ yard
  Interior: 1   12" × 18"
  Exterior: 1   12¾" × 18¾"
  Lid: 1   6¾" × 12¾"
Cardboard: ¼" thick
  Box: 1   12" × 18"
  Lid: 1   6½" × 12½"
X-Acto knife
Metal-edge ruler
Masking tape
Glue
Batting:
  Interior: 2   11¾" × 2¾"
        2   5¾" × 2¾"
        1   5¾" × 11¾" (base)
  Exterior: 2   12" × 3"
        2   6" × 3"
  Lid: 1   6½" × 12½"

Instructions: Select a 6-inch-square design. Piece 2 blocks as directed in the individual instructions. Sew the blocks together, matching seams carefully.

First prepare the cardboard box. Following the cardboard diagram (Fig. 191), measure and mark a 3-inch-square in each corner of the large cardboard rectangle. Continue drawing the lines across the cardboard, 3 inches in from the edges, following the dot/dash lines on the diagram. Using an X-Acto knife and a metal-edge ruler, cut away the 3-inch corner squares, indicated by the shaded areas on the diagram. Next, score the cardboard on each of the dot/dash lines. To score, place the ruler exactly on the line and run the X-Acto knife along the edge of the ruler, cutting approximately halfway through the cardboard; do not cut all the way through. Bend the cardboard along the score lines to form a box; tape the corners together securely.

Attach the batting next. Glue the long and short interior strips inside the box along the sides, then glue the base rectangle in place. Glue the exterior strips of batting to the outside of the box along the sides; the exterior base does not require padding. Glue the remaining piece of batting to one side of the cardboard lid.

Next make the fabric covering. For the interior, cut away a 3-inch square from each corner of the fabric as you did for the cardboard. Stitch the cor-

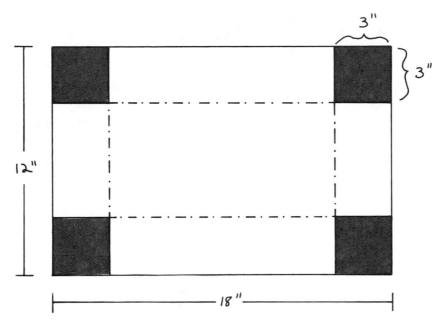

Fig. 191 Treasure Box cardboard diagram

ner edges together making ¼-inch seams, forming a fabric "box." Insert inside the padded cardboard box with wrong sides facing the batting; smooth neatly in place. For the exterior, cut away a 2¾-inch square from each corner of the fabric. Stitch the corner edges together making ¼-inch seams as you did for the interior; turn right-side out. Insert the cardboard box inside the fabric "box," smoothing and wrapping the fabric neatly over the cardboard; the fit should be snug. Fold the edges of the fabrics over one another at the top edge of the box and slip-stitch together securely, hiding all raw edges.

For the lid, stitch the backing fabric to the pieced blocks, leaving one long edge open for the back edge; ease the backing fabric to fit the edges of the pieced blocks. Turn right side out and press. Insert the cardboard lid inside the pocket just made so the padded side is beneath the pieced top. Fold the edges of the fabrics over one another at the back of the lid and slip-stitch together, hiding all raw edges.

To finish, sew the back edge of the lid to the back edge of the box with sturdy slip-stitches.

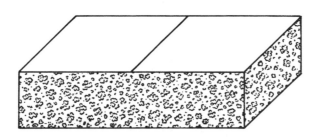

Fig. 192 Treasure Box assembly diagram

Geometric Wall Hanging

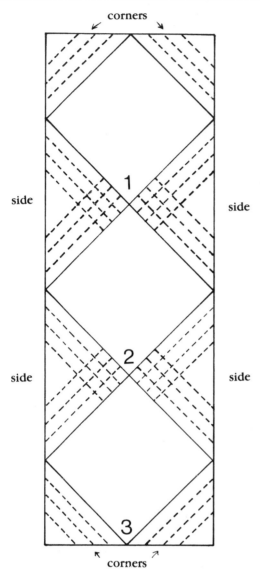

corners

side   side

side   side

corners

Fig. 193   Geometric Wall Hanging assembly diagram

Finished size: 14½" × 43"

Requirements

Pieced blocks: 3   10" square—¼ yard pale, ⅛ yard each of 4 to 5 assorted fabrics

Background (right angle triangles): 4 sides 10½" × 10½" × 14¼"; 4 corners 7⅜" × 7⅜" × 10½" —½ yard dark fabric (includes fabric for pieced blocks)

Back: 1   15½" × 44" —½ yard dark (includes fabric for sleeve)

Binding: self-binding

Sleeve: 1   14½" × 2"

Create a patchwork of modern art to hang in your home—the shape is ideal for brightening up a narrow space in a hallway or along a stairway. The optical illusion of overlapping and "interweaving" is very easy to achieve. Use bright solid fabrics for a bold effect.

Select 3 geometric designs from the 4 given on the following pages; piece as directed in the individual instructions. (*Note:* You may notice that the blocks have been pieced slightly differently in the photograph and the diagrams; this is because I reworked the designs after the project was finished to simplify them. The finished effect will still be the same—you'll just have an easier time piecing than I did!)

After the blocks have been completed, sew the corner triangles to blocks 1 and 3. Sew a side triangle to the upper left and lower right edge of block 2. Then sew a side triangle to the lower right edge of block 1 and the upper left edge of block 3. Matching seams carefully, sew the 3 strips just made together.

See *Assembling a Project for Quilting* and assemble the wall hanging as directed. Quilt the blocks following the individual instructions. Quilt the side triangles and corners with overlapping parallel lines as shown on the assembly diagram. Self-bind the project as directed in *Binding a Project*.

See *Hanging a Patchwork Project*; make and attach a sleeve or strap as directed. The project can also be used as a table runner.

INTERLOCKED SQUARES

Challenging
Pieces per block: 29

A	1 pale	E	4 bright
B	4 bright	F	4 dark
C	4 dark	G	8 pale
D	4 bright		

A geometric puzzle, this dramatic design looks striking in bright bold shades. Careful matching of seams is required to achieve the lovely interlocked effect. Each of the corners is mitred; see *How to Mitre Corners*.

Fig. 194   Interlocked Squares

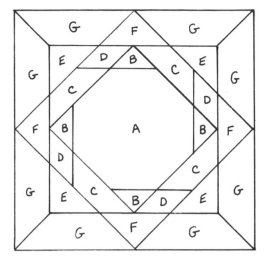

Fig. 195   Interlaced Star

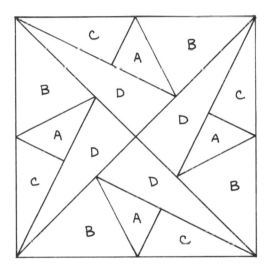

Templates are on page 104. To begin, sew a B to each side edge of A. Sew each D to the right edge of C as shown in the diagram. Sew C-D to each A-B edge, matching D to B. Sew E to each C-D edge.

For the outer edges, sew G to each side of each F. Sew G-F-G to each side of the central square, matching the edges of F to the outer edges of C and D. Mitre each of the corners to complete the design.

Outline-quilt the bright and dark pieces using matching quilting thread.

INTERLACED STAR

Moderate
Pieces per block: 16

A	1 light, 1 bright, 1 medium, 1 dark	C	4 pale
		D	1 light, 1 bright, 1 medium, 1 dark
B	4 pale		

A wonderful feeling of motion and excitement is created by this design. Careful marking and cutting are essential, as is careful placement of the fabrics. To avoid confusion, arrange all the cut

103

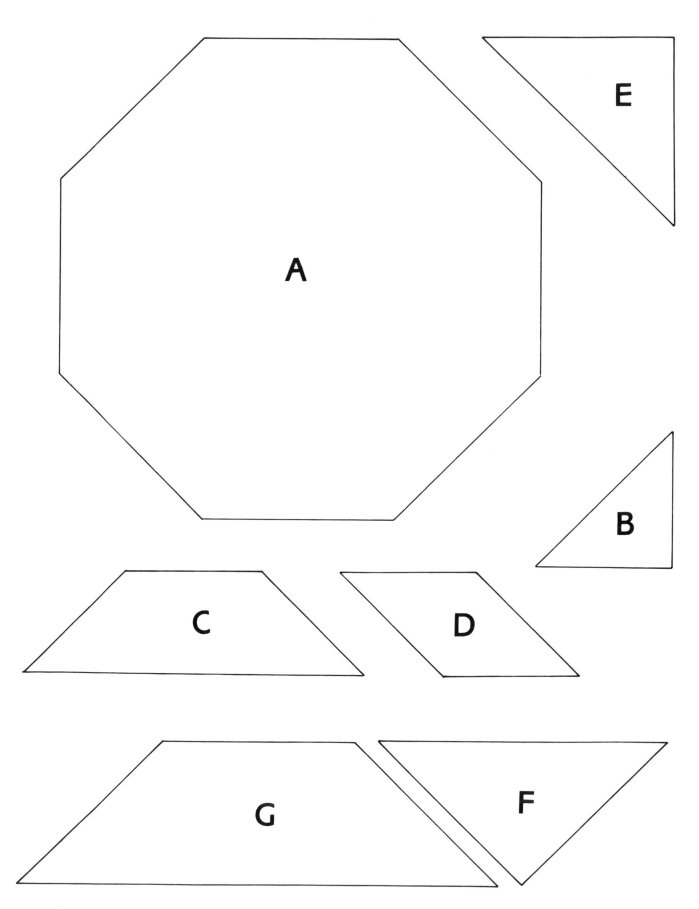

Fig. 196   Interlocked Squares templates

104

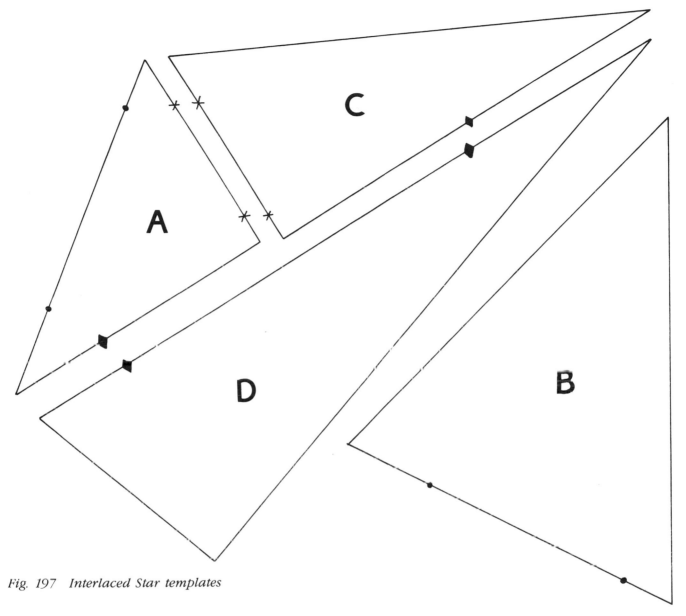

Fig. 197 Interlaced Star templates

pieces on a flat surface, then separate the pieces into 4 triangles; assemble each of the four triangles in the same way.

To begin, sew A to B, matching the dots. Then sew A to C, matching the crosses. Sew A-C to D, matching the notches.

To assemble the block, sew 2 pairs of triangles together to form each half of the design; press the seam allowances in opposite directions. Sew the halves together, matching seams carefully in the middle, to complete the design.

Outline-quilt the star on the pale fabric all around each of the pieces. Quilt across the middle of the star making an X; use quilting thread to match the fabrics you are quilting.

INTERWOVEN LINES

Easy

Pieces per block: 42

A	1 light	G	1 pale, 1 bright, 1 medium
B	2 dark		
C	2 pale, 1 bright, 2 dark	H	1 pale, 1 bright, 1 medium
D	4 pale, 1 bright, 3 medium, 4 dark	J	3 bright, 4 medium, 2 dark
E	1 pale	K	1 pale, 1 medium
F	2 pale, 1 bright, 1 medium		

While there are a lot of pieces in this block, it is all straight and easy sewing—a good way for a

105

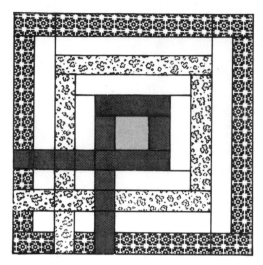

Fig. 198   Interwoven Lines

beginner to practice matching seams and following diagrams and instructions. The block is assembled from the middle outward in rounds; take your time to get the colors right.

To begin, sew a B to opposite sides of A. Sew a dark C to each B-A-B edge. For the second round, sew a pale C to the right edge of the middle. Sew a dark D to E; sew to the left edge of the middle. Sew a pale F to the top. Sew a dark D between a pale D and pale C; sew the strip just made to the bottom.

For the next round, sew a bright F to the right edge of the middle. Sew a dark D between a bright D and a bright C; sew to the left edge of the middle. Sew a bright H to the top. Sew a dark D between a bright G and a bright J; sew to the bottom, matching seams carefully.

The outer two rounds are sewn together before being sewn to the middle, beginning with the top and bottom, then the sides. For the top, sew a pale H to a medium H; sew the pale H to the bright H of the middle. For the bottom of the round, sew a pale D to a medium D and a pale G to a medium G. Sew a dark J in between D-D and G-G, keeping the medium pieces aligned along the same edge. Sew a bright J to the remaining D-D edge. Sew the strip just made to the bottom, with the medium pieces along the outer edge.

For the left side, it is important to keep the medium pieces aligned along the outer edge. Sew a pale F to a medium F; sew a medium J to the top

of F-F as shown and then sew a dark J to the bottom of F-F. Sew each remaining pale D to a medium D, making 2 pairs. Sew one pair to the dark J; sew the other pair between a medium and a bright J. Sew the bright J edge to the remaining D-D edge; sew the strip just made to the left side of the block. For the right side, sew the K's together; sew a J to each end. Sew the pale K to the right edge of the block to complete the design.

Outline-quilt each of the colored "lines" with matching thread.

INTERLOCKED BLOCKS

Moderate
Pieces per block: 20

A	4 light, 2 pale,	B	1 pale, 1 bright,
	2 bright,		1 medium, 1 dark
	2 medium, 2 dark	C	4 light

Also known as Card Trick, this design is constructed with a central square and 4 pieced rectangles. Take care to match seams for a crisp geometric effect.

Templates are on page 108. Arrange the cut pieces on a flat surface following the diagram to get the best color mix. Separate the pieces into one central square surrounded by 4 rectangles. Sew the 4 central A's together, first in pairs, then in halves to complete the middle square.

To make each of the rectangles, sew the 2 A's together, making a right-angle triangle; sew A-A to one edge of B. Sew C to the opposite edge of B.

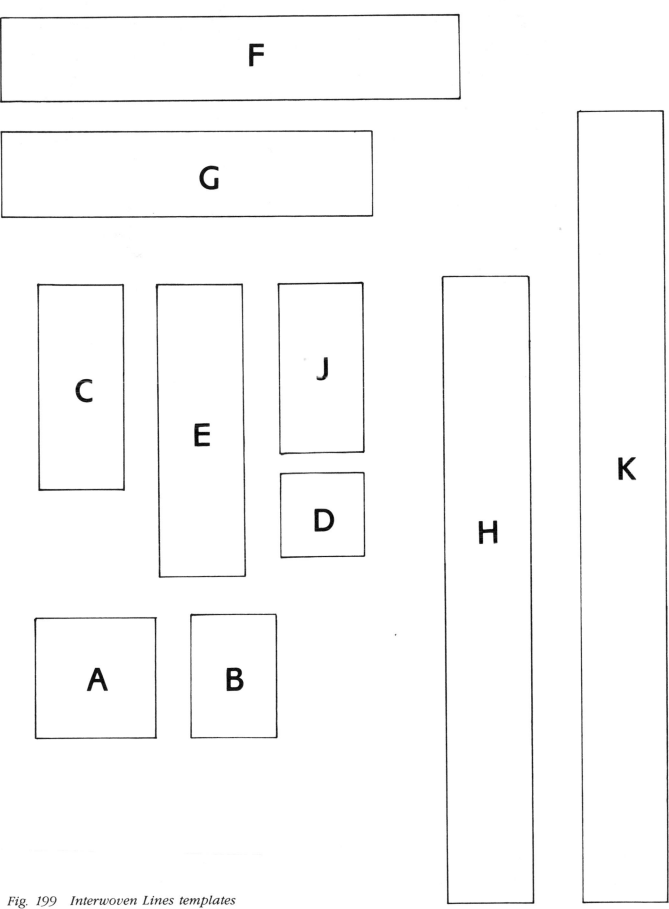

Fig. 199   Interwoven Lines templates

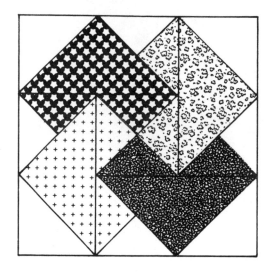
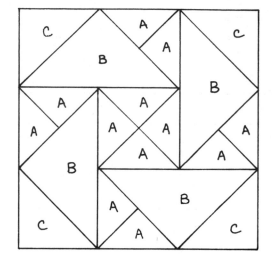

Fig. 200   *Interlocked Blocks*

Arrange the rectangles around the central square as shown in the diagram. Place the first rectangle, right sides together against the central square— the rectangle will be flush with the square at one edge, and will extend beyond the square at the other. Sew from the flush edge halfway across the central square; stop your stitching. Sew the next rectangle in place to the straight edge just created.

Repeat in a clockwise fashion for the next 2 rectangles, pressing as you go. Return to the first seam which was sewn only halfway—you now have a straight edge to sew the extension to. Stitch the remainder of that seam to complete the design.

Outline-quilt each of the 4 "blocks" using matching quilting thread.

Fig. 201   *Interlocked Blocks templates*

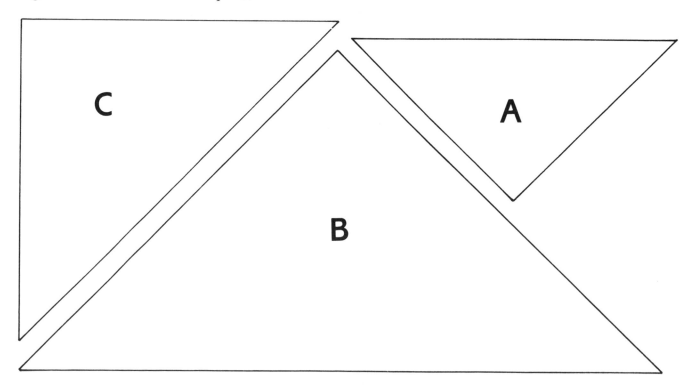

Patchwork in a Hoop

Fig. 202

Make a simple yet appealing picture for your wall—already framed in its own hoop! Add some pretty quilting around the edges and an embroidered message to surprise a friend with a very special gift.

Before beginning, review the following sections: *Embroidery*, and *Assembling a Project for Quilting*.

Easy
Finished size: 14" diameter
Requirements
Pieced block: 1 6" square—fabric scraps or ⅛ yard each of 3 to 5 fabrics
Frame: ¾ yard (includes fabric for lining)
  Short: 2 6½" square
  Long: 2 6½" × 18½"
  Lining: 1 16" diameter circle (cut this before cutting the pieces for the frame)
Back (for quilting): 1 18"-diameter circle—½ yard
Batting: 18"-diameter circle
Hoop: 14"-diameter circular wooden hoop
6-strand embroidery floss
Large hook (from a hook and eye pair)

Instructions: Select a 6-inch-square design. Piece as directed in the individual instructions.

Sew a short frame to the top and bottom of the block; press carefully. Sew a long frame to each side.

If you are planning to add an embroidered message, practice writing the message on scrap paper first, then position the paper around the block to test the fit. When satisfied with your result, write the message in pencil on the frame, or transfer your practice writing to the frame using carbon paper and a hard lead pencil. Embroider the message in outline stitch, using 6 strands of floss in your needle.

Assemble the framed patchwork for quilting as directed in *Assembling a Project for Quilting*. Quilt the block following the individual instructions. Use the quilting design (Fig. 204) to quilt the frame; the dot matches up to the middle of one side of the block.

When the quilting has been completed, trim the excess fabric extending beyond the hoop on the back to a 1-inch seam allowance. Finger-press the raw edges towards the middle of the back.

Press the raw edges of the lining 1 inch to the wrong side, easing as necessary to achieve a smoothly-curved edge. Pin the pressed edge over the seam allowance of the quilted front so all raw edges are hidden inside. Slip-stitch the pressed edge invisibly in place. Sew a hook to the back for hanging.

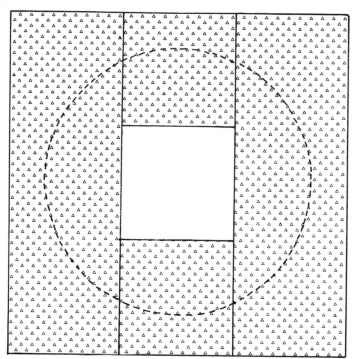

*Fig. 203 Patchwork in a Hoop
assembly diagram*

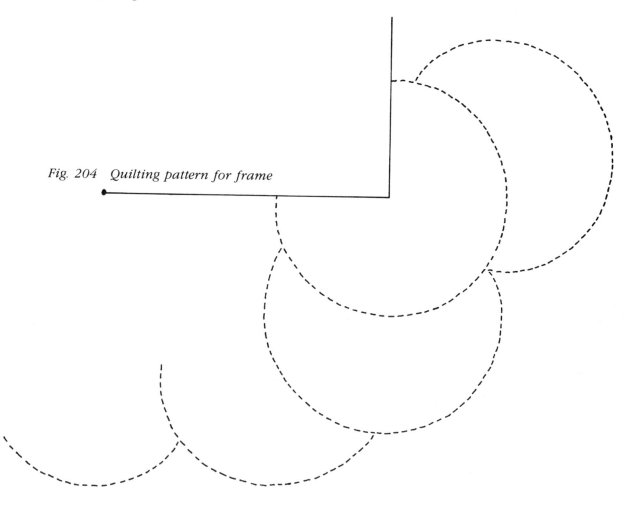

Fig. 204 Quilting pattern for frame

GIFTS

Sachet

Place pretty Sachets in your bureau drawers and suitcases to freshen your clothes. Filled with potpourri, the scent will linger for many months. When the Sachets are no longer "doing their job," refill with new potpourri or spray with a potpourri revitalizer.

Easy
Size: 4" square
Requirements
Pieced block: 1 4" square—fabric scraps
Back: 1 4½" square—fabric scrap
Ruffled lace trim: ½" wide—½ yard
Potpourri

Instructions: The following 6-inch-square block designs contain 2- or 4-inch-square elements:

Belt Buckle
Broken Dishes
Coming of Spring
Contrary Wife
Devil's Advocate
Dutch Treat
English Thistle

Flower Cross
Love in a Mist
Quandary
Roundabout
Single Wedding Ring
Spring Blossom

Fig. 205

Fig. 206

Study these blocks to isolate the 2- or 4-inch-square elements, then select one that you like. Use the templates to cut the appropriate number of pieces needed to create a 4-inch square. Piece as directed in the individual instructions.

You will find that by turning the pieces in various ways or by re-using one 2-inch element 4 times, you'll create hundreds of designs. For example, the sachet shown in the photograph is composed of a 2-inch-square element found in Devil's Advocate and Coming of Spring (the B-D-B square).

Have fun and experiment—you'll be amazed at the number of different designs you'll create.

When the 4-inch square is complete, sew the ruffled lace trim in place all around the edges as directed in *Lace.*

Sew the pieced front to the back with right sides facing and the ruffled lace trim sandwiched in between; leave a 1½-inch opening on one side for turning. Clip off each of the corners, then turn right-side out. Fill with potpourri until plump. Turn the raw edges at the opening ¼ inch to the inside and slip-stitch closed.

Jewelry Bag

Fig. 207

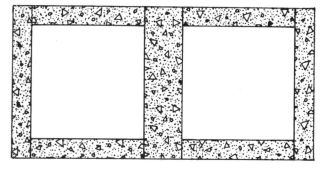

Fig. 208

Protect your jewelry when travelling by storing it in this padded case. The case can also be used for packing stockings or delicate lingerie. This project would make an excellent and unusual bazaar or craft-fair item—if quilted by machine, you should be able to complete one in just a few hours.

Before beginning, review the following sections: *Assembling a Project for Quilting*, and *Binding a Project*.

Moderate
Finished size: About 8" square
Requirements
Pieced blocks: 2 6" square—fabric scraps
Remainder of bag: ¼ yard (includes fabric for background of each pieced block)
Borders: 2 1½" × 6½"; 2 1½" × 8½"
Central panel: 1 2½" × 8½"
Back: 8½" × 16½"—scrap muslin
Binding: 2 1" × 9"—fabric scrap
Zipper: 1 6" long—neutral color

Instructions: Select a 6-inch-square design; piece 2 blocks as directed in the individual instructions. Sew a short border to the top and bottom edges of each block. Sew the blocks to each side of the central panel. Sew the remaining borders to each side edge of the project.

See *Assembling a Project for Quilting*; assemble the project as directed. Quilt the blocks following the individual instructions. If desired, quilt parallel lines at regular intervals across the borders and central panel.

Fold the raw edges at each short end ¼ inch to the wrong side. Pin the folded edges to the right side of the zipper, placing the folds about ⅛ inch away from each side of the zipper's teeth; slip-stitch each folded edge securely to the zipper.

The project is now a tube—with the ends connected at the zipper. Smooth the project flat so it is folded in half in the middle of the central panel; baste the open edges together. At the zipper end, roll the edges with your fingers so the zipper is ¼ inch below the fold, and thus invisible from the outside. Quilt along the top edge of each of the folds just made, securing the zipper inside the bag.

Review *Binding a Project* for instructions on making and attaching the binding. Bind each side edge of the jewelry bag, folding the ends under neatly to finish.

112

Evening Bag

Fig. 209

Make a fashion statement by carrying this simple yet elegant Evening Bag on your next night on the town. There are 2 styles from which to choose—the patchwork bag can be made in an array of dazzling silks, while the plain quilted bag can show off a treasured piece of fabric.

I'd like to thank Sharon Falberg, an American currently living in London, for allowing me to use her design in this book. She also made the evening bag shown in Color Illus. 16B, using a lovely piece of silk that she bought in Japan.

Moderate

Finished size: About 5½" × 6½" (excluding strap)

Requirements

*Front: scraps of 4 different fabrics such as silk or polyester for the patchwork bag, **OR** 1 6" × 7" piece of printed silk or polyester for the plain quilted bag*

Back: 1 6" × 7" piece of fabric to coordinate with the front

Batting: 1 5½" × 6½"

Strap: 1 1" × 36" (or desired length) to match back

Lining: 2 6" × 7" pieces of lining fabric

Loop: 1 1" × 3½" to match strap

Button: 1 ½" diameter

Instructions: To make the patchwork bag, use the templates to cut the following pieces:

A	1 dark	C	1 bright,
B	1 medium,		1 bright reversed
	1 medium reversed	D	1 light, 1 light reversed

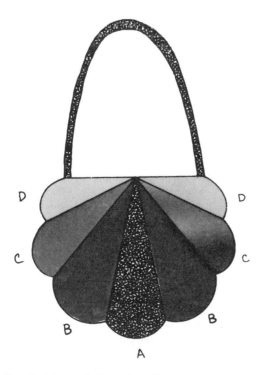

Fig. 210   Patchwork Evening Bag

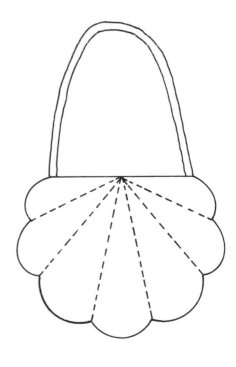

Fig. 211   Plain Quilted Evening Bag

113

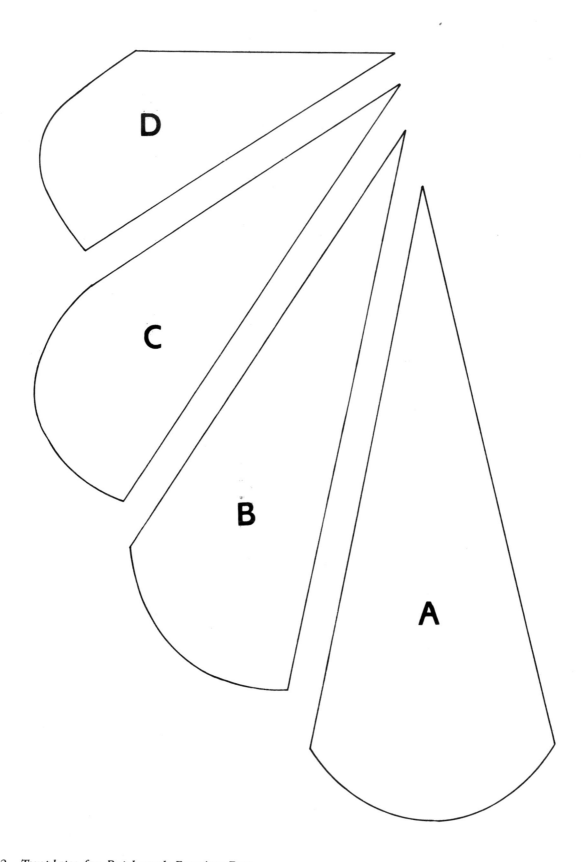

Fig. 212   Templates for Patchwork Evening Bag

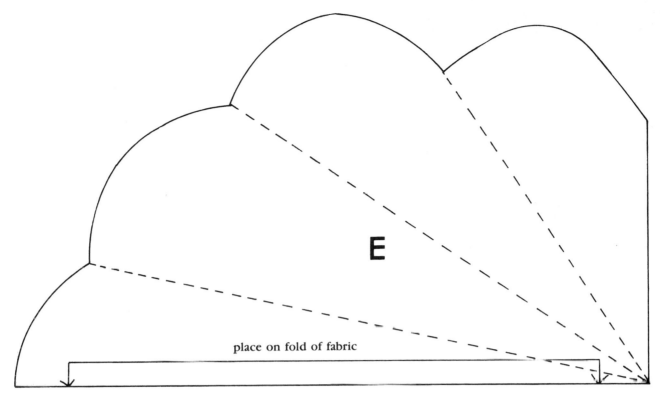

place on fold of fabric

Fig. 213   Template for Plain Quilted Evening Bag

Sew a B to each side of A. Sew a C to each B, then sew a D to each C.

To make the plain quilted bag, use template E to cut one piece from your chosen fabric, placing the straight edge of the pattern on the fold. Using chalk, lightly mark the quilting lines on the right side of the fabric.

From this point, the instructions are the same for both the patchwork and the plain quilted bags.

Baste the batting to the wrong side of the front. Quilt along each of the seam lines or the marked quilting lines. Trim the batting even with the edges of the top. With right sides facing and raw edges even, stitch the front to the back, sewing smoothly around the curves and angling your stitches sharply at each point. Clip into the seam allowance along the curves and just to the stitching line at each point. Turn right side out and press very gently so as not to affect the batting. Fold the raw top edges ¼ inch to the inside; baste in place all around.

Fold the strap in half lengthwise with right sides facing; stitch the long edges together. Turn right side out using a tube turner. Press carefully, then topstitch close to each long edge. Pin the ends inside the bag, ⅜ inch below the folded top edges on each side; slip-stitch invisibly in place.

Use template E to cut 2 lining pieces, placing the straight edge of the pattern on the fold. Stitch together with right sides facing and raw edges even in the same way you stitched the front and back together. Clip the seam allowances in the same way. Do not turn right side out. Press the raw top edges ¼ inch to the wrong side (outside).

Insert the lining inside the bag, wrong sides facing and with the side seams matching; pin together around the top with the folded edges even and the straps in between. Slip-stitch the top edges together all around. Remove the basting.

See *Loops & Ties* for instructions on making the loop. Fold the raw ends under twice and slip-stitch in place. Slip-stitch the ends of the loop to the lining along the upper middle edge of the back. Sew the button to the front along the upper middle edge. Secure the loop around the button to close the bag.

115

Tote Bag

Fig. 214

I have come to the conclusion that the most common factor in the world's everyday wardrobe is a plastic bag—usually promoting the name of a local supermarket or shoe store, and filled with necessities that simply couldn't be left at home. Until I became involved with patchwork, I must confess that I was the greatest user of these plastic bags (and was often called "the bag lady" by my colleagues). I always defended myself by saying that you never know when you'll get stuck on a train and will need a good book, or when you'll get hungry and must have an orange, or when your shoes will begin to pinch and you'll need another pair . . . well, you get the picture.

This Tote Bag is so much more attractive than any plastic bag and takes so little time to make, you'll wonder why you ever let yourself become a walking advertisement! It is quite large and roomy; if you carry it on your shoulder, it will wrap comfortably around the side of your body, making it very unobtrusive.

Before beginning, review the following sections: *Assembling a Project for Quilting, Machine Quilting, Binding a Project,* and *Loops & Ties.*

Easy

Size: About 20" square

Requirements

Pieced blocks: 4   6" square—yardage included with fabrics used for remainder of bag; use scraps to fill in extra colors

Remainder of bag: ¾ yard light, ⅜ yard bright, ¼ yard dark

> *Front*
>> *Lattice (bright): 4   1¼" × 6½"; 4   1¼" × 13¼"*
>> *Squares (dark): 5   1¼" square*
>> *Corner right-angle triangles (light): 4   10¾" × 10¾" × 15"*
> *Back (of bag)*
>> *Middle (light): 1   17" square*
>> *Border (bright): 4   2" × 17"*
>> *Corners: 4   2" square*

Binding (bright): 5   1" × 21"

Braid: 2   1" × 97" light; 2   1" × 97" bright; 2   1" × 97" dark

Piping cord: ¼" diameter—16½ yards

Back (for quilting): 2   21" square—⅝ yard muslin

Batting: 2   21" square

Loop: 1   1" × 4"

Button: 1   ⅝" diameter

Instructions: For the front of the bag, select a 6-inch-square design. Piece 4 blocks following the individual instructions. Sew a block to each long edge of 2 short lattices. Sew the remaining short lattices to opposite sides of a dark square. Sew the block/lattice strips to each side of the pieced lattice, matching seams carefully. Sew a long lattice to each side of the pieced middle. Sew a square to each end of the remaining long lattices; sew to the top and bottom of the pieced middle. Sew a corner triangle to each edge of the pieced middle to complete the front of the bag.

For the back of the bag, sew a border to each side of the light square. Sew a corner to each end of the remaining 2 borders; sew to the top and bottom of the square. Using a pencil or erasable marker, sketch a quilting design in the middle of

116

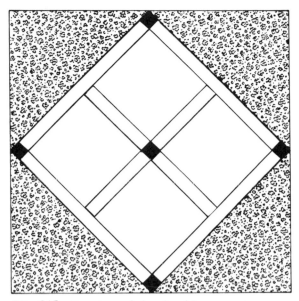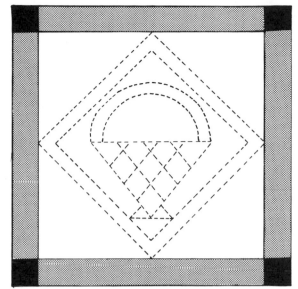

Fig. 215 Front and back of bag

the light square; follow the design given in the assembly diagram or make up a design of your own.

See *Assembling a Project for Quilting*. Assemble the front and back as directed. On the front, quilt the blocks following the individual instructions; outline-quilt each of the lattices. On the back, quilt the marked design by hand or machine; outline-quilt the borders and corners.

Trim the batting and muslin even with the front and back. See *Binding a Project*; bind the top edges of the front and back.

Pin the front to the back matching all edges and trimming the sides and bottom to match if necessary. Bind the bottom, then the side edges together, folding the raw ends under at each side edge to finish neatly.

To make the braid, piece the fabrics as necessary to create the 97-inch strips. For a ragged braid, simply press each of the strips in half, wrong sides inward, place a 97-inch length of piping cord in-

side each strip and stitch close to the cord to hold it in place. For a smooth braid, stitch the long edges of each strip together and turn right side out using a tube turner; insert a 97-inch length of piping cord inside each tube using a tube turner. Fold the raw ends ¼ inch inside and slip-stitch together. Holding a light, bright, and dark strip with their ends even, knot together about ½ inch from the end. Braid the strips together firmly; knot at the other end, leaving ½-inch tails. Repeat for the other braid.

Starting at the base of the front, pin the braid up the front, close to the side edge. Slip-stitch in place securely from bottom to top. Repeat with the other end of the same braid along the opposite edge of the front. Repeat on the back in the same manner.

See *Loops & Ties* for instructions on making the loop. Stitch the ends of the loop to the inside of the back at the midpoint. Sew a button to the right side of the front in the middle of the top square. Secure the loop around the button to close the bag.

Shoe Tote

Fig. 216

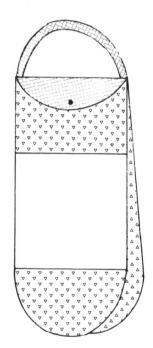

Fig. 217

and will not become dirty easily. There is one compartment for each shoe. The bag can be made to fit any shoe size—for men or for women.

Before beginning, review *Binding a Project* and *Buttonholes*.

Moderate
Finished size: About 6" × 14"
Requirements
Pieced blocks: 2   6" square—scraps **OR** *⅛ yard each of 3 to 5 fabrics*
Remainder of bag: ⅜ to ½ yard (depending on shoe size)
  Top: 2   4¼" × 6½" (adjust 4¼" measurement if shoe is longer than 13")
  Toe: 2   (using template)
  Flaps: 4   (using template)
  Sides: 2   3½" × 30½" (3½" measurement is height of shoe; measure height of your shoe, flat on a surface to determine correct width; for high heels, measure height of shoe on its side)
  Strap: 1   1½" × 15"
  Top Binding: 2   1¼" × 6½"
          4   1¼" × 3½" (or width of side)
  Side Binding: 3   1¼" × 31"
Lining: ½ yard denim or sturdy fabric
Buttons: 2   ½" diameter

Instructions: Select a 6-inch-square block design. Piece 2 blocks as directed in the individual instructions.

Sew the top and toe pieces to opposite edges of each block. Press carefully. Use one pieced front as a pattern to cut 4 linings from the denim. Also cut 2 side pieces from the denim, each 3½" × 30½" (or the width of your side pieces).

With wrong sides facing, stitch each pieced front to a lining, and stitch each side to a lining. Bind the straight top edge of each front, and the short edges of each side as directed in *Binding a Project*.

With lining sides facing and raw edges even, pin each front to a side, easing around the curves and matching the bound top edges. Stitch together ⅛ inch from the edges all around, then bind each seam, folding the ends under neatly to finish.

With right sides facing and curved edges even, sew 2 pairs of flaps together; turn right side out and press. Topstitch the raw edges together. Make

My long-suffering husband (who puts up with thread on his suits, pins in his feet and regular Wednesday quilting meetings in our home) asked me to make him a bag in which he could carry his golf shoes. Pleased to be able to make something that I knew he wanted, I designed this Shoe Tote. It's lined with denim so the inside is very sturdy

2 ⅝-inch vertical buttonhole in the middle of each flap, ¼ inch above the curved edge.

For the strap, stitch the long edges together with right sides facing. Turn right side out using a tube turner, and press. Pin the ends of the strap to each side edge of one flap, with raw straight edges even and right sides facing; baste in place. Baste the flaps together with right sides facing and the strap sandwiched in between, along the straight edge. Pin the flaps, centered, to the straight edge of one of the remaining linings on the right side. Pin the linings together, with right sides facing and the flaps and strap sandwiched in between. Stitch together across the straight top edge, making small stitches. Turn right side out and press so one flap folds down on each lining, and the strap hangs free. Stitch the edges of the linings together; this completes the central lining.

Pin the remaining edges of the sides to each side of the central lining, easing around the curves. Stitch together making a ⅛-inch seam, then bind the seam, folding the ends under neatly to finish.

Place a shoe in each compartment and fold the flap over the pieced front to mark the position for each button. Sew a button to each front in the marked position.

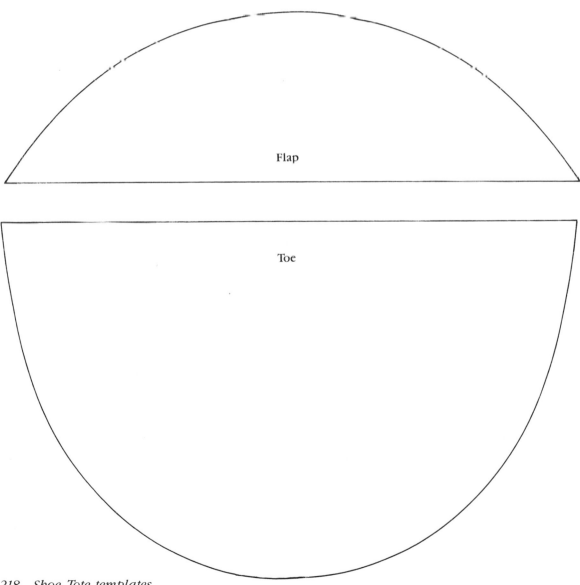

Fig. 218   Shoe Tote templates

Picnic Set

This is truly a scrap project—and one that you'll use time and again when you and your family go on a picnic. It is an easy and fast way to use up all your fabric scraps. Backed with sturdy denim, the blanket and cushions are extremely practical. There are no templates; you simply sew fabric strips to muslin squares, then sew the squares together—it's as simple as that. Be sure to pre-wash the muslin and denim.

Before beginning, review the following sections: *Rotary Cutting*, *Machine Quilting*, and *Binding a Project*.

Easy
Size: 36" × 48" blanket; 24" square cushions
    (instructions are given for 4 cushions)
Requirements
Pieced blocks: 28   12" square—fabric scraps cut into long strips ¾" to 2½" wide
    Back (for pieced blocks): 28   12½" square—3⅓ yards muslin
Back: 1   36½" × 48½" for blanket; 4   24½" square for cushions—4⅛ yards sturdy denim
Binding (for blanket): 1½" × 95"—fabric scraps (if pieced) **OR** *⅛ yard (if using solid fabric)*
Thick batting (for cushions): 8   24" square

Instructions: For each pieced square, place a fabric strip, right side up, diagonally across the middle of a muslin square; pin each edge in place. Place a second fabric strip, right side down and long edges even, over the first strip; stitch the strips together making a ¼-inch seam. Turn the second strip over to the right side and press. Place a third strip, face down, over the first strip, matching the remaining long raw edges; stitch together. Turn to the right side and press. Continue stitching and pressing fabric strips to the muslin square in this way until the entire square is covered; press carefully. Turn the pieced block over to the wrong (muslin) side; trim away the ragged edges of the fabric strips even with the edges of the muslin. Baste around the outer edge of the block. Each block is assembled in the same way.

BLANKET

After you have completed 12 blocks, arrange them on a flat surface in 4 rows, with 3 squares in each row. Allow the strips on the blocks to slant in the same direction as shown in the diagram, or turn the blocks in random directions as you wish. Try to get a good mix of colors across the blanket. When satisfied with your arrangement, sew the blocks together in 4 rows with 3 blocks in each row; make no attempt to match the pieced seams of the blocks—a random effect is desired.

Sew the rows together, this time matching the seams only at the corners of the blocks; press carefully.

With wrong sides facing, baste the denim back to the blanket. Machine-quilt along the major seams, then quilt other seams at random.

Review *Binding a Project* for instructions on making and attaching a binding. A pieced binding is illustrated, but you can use a solid binding to save time. Bind the blanket all around, mitring the corners.

CUSHIONS

After you have completed 16 blocks, arrange them on a flat surface in 4 groups of 4. Angle the strips on the blocks as shown in the assembly diagram, or turn the blocks in random directions as you wish. Try to get a good mix of colors in each cushion. When satisfied with your arrangement, sew the blocks together in pairs, then sew the pairs together, matching seams in the middle to complete each cushion; press carefully.

Baste 2 squares of thick batting to the wrong side of each pieced top. Machine-quilt along the angled seams of each block.

With right sides facing and raw edges even, pin each cushion top to a denim back around all edges. Stitch together all around, leaving a 4" opening along one edge for turning. Clip off the corners at an angle, then turn right side out through the opening. Fold the raw edges at the opening ¼" inside and slip-stitch closed.

Fig. 219 Cushion

Fig. 220 Blanket

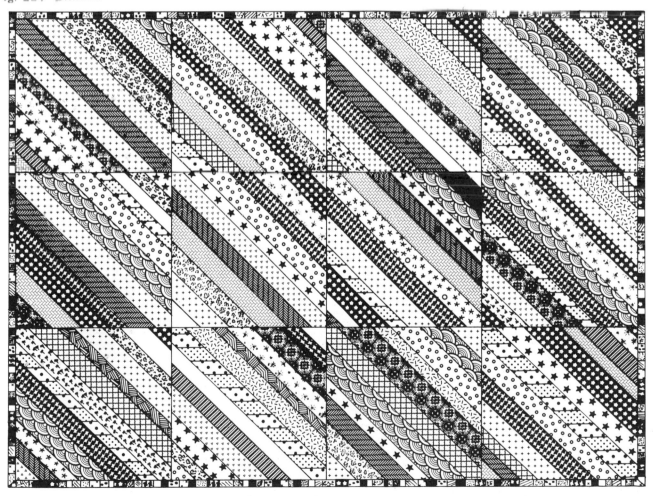

Fig. 221

WINE TOTE

Carry your favorite bottle of wine in this padded wine tote and you'll never run the risk of breaking it. Made from scrap fabrics, this project can easily be made in about 1½ hours. Before beginning, review the following sections: *Rotary Cutting* and *Quilt-As-You-Go*.

Easy
Size: 8" high (excluding strap)
Requirements
Pieced block: 1   8" × 12"—fabric scraps cut into long strips ¾" to 2½" wide
Back (of block) and lining: 2   8½" × 12½" —¼ yard muslin
Base: 2   3½" diameter—muslin
Strap: 2   1¾" × 13"—fabric scrap
Batting: 1   8" × 12"; 1   3" diameter

Instructions: For the pieced block, baste the rectangle of batting to the middle of the muslin back. Place a fabric strip, right side up, diagonally across the middle of the batting; pin each edge in place. Place a second fabric strip, right side down and long edges even, over the first strip; stitch the strips together along one edge, making a ¼-inch seam. Turn the second strip to the right side and "finger-press" the seam by running your index finger over the seam several times. (Do not press or the iron may melt the batting.) Place a third strip, right side down, over the first strip, matching the remaining long raw edge; stitch together. Turn right side out

Fig. 222

base

Fig. 223   *Wine Tote assembly diagram*

pieced block

strap

and finger-press in place. Continue stitching and finger-pressing the fabric strips to the batting and muslin rectangle in this way until the entire rectangle is covered. Turn the pieced block over to the wrong (muslin) side; trim away the ragged edges of the fabric strips even with the edges of the muslin. Baste around the outer edge of the block. Stitch the short edges together with right sides facing, forming a tube.

For the base, center the batting on one muslin circle and baste in place. Stitch strips of fabric over the batting in the same way as for the pieced block; trim the edges even with the circle when finished. Machine-baste all around the edge. Gently pull the basting stitches, gathering the edges of the base to fit one end of the tube. Pin, then stitch the base to the tube with right sides facing.

Pin the 2 strap pieces together with right sides facing and raw edges even; stitch along each long edge. Turn right side out and press; topstitch the long edges. Pin each end of the strap to the top of the tube at opposite edges, with right sides facing and raw edges even, baste in place.

For the lining, stitch the short edges of the remaining muslin rectangle together; press. With right sides facing and the straps sandwiched in between, slide the muslin tube inside the pieced tube so the raw edges are even at the top; stitch together all around. Turn right side out, exposing the straps, so the lining side is on the outside of the tube. Topstitch ¼ inch from the top edges all around. Smooth the lining over the inside of the tube and baste the edges together at the bottom seam. Machine-baste around the edge of the remaining muslin circle; gather to fit the end of the tube, then press the raw edges ¼ inch to the wrong side. With wrong sides facing, pin the circle over the seam at the base, covering all raw edges. Slip-stitch in place, then turn the wine tote right side out.

UTENSILS HOLDER

Store your silverware or picnic supplies in this handy utensils holder. The top of the holder folds down, and then the project rolls and ties, enclosing all your pieces securely. Before beginning, read the following sections: *Rotary Cutting*, *Binding a Project*, and *Loops & Ties*.

Easy
Size: 8" × 12" (unrolled)

Requirements

Pieced blocks: 1   12" square; 1   6" × 12"—fabric scraps cut into long strips ¾" × 2½" wide
Back: 1   12½" square; 1   6½" × 12½"—⅜ yard muslin
Lining: 1   6½" × 12½"—muslin
Binding: 4   1" × 12½"—⅛ yard (includes fabric for tie)
Tie: 1   1" × 18"

Instructions: For each pieced block, place a fabric strip, right side up, diagonally across the middle of the muslin back; pin each edge in place. Place

Fig. 225   Utensils Holder assembly diagram

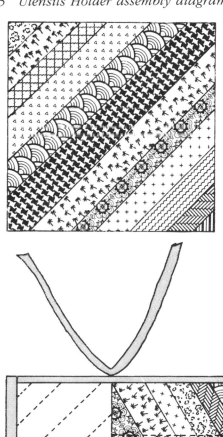

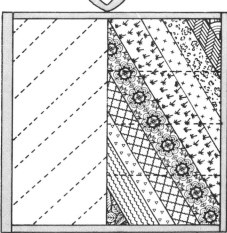

a second fabric strip, right side down and long edges even, over the first strip; stitch the strips together along one edge, making a ¼-inch seam. Turn the second strip to the right side and press. Place a third strip, right side down, over the first strip, matching the remaining long raw edge; stitch together. Turn to the right side and press. Continue stitching and pressing the fabric strips to the muslin back in this way until the entire back is covered. Turn the pieced block over to the wrong (muslin) side; trim away the ragged edges of the fabric strips even with the edges of the muslin. Baste around the outer edge of the block.

With right sides facing, stitch the lining to the small pieced block along one long edge; turn right side out and press. Topstitch close to the edge.

With the muslin sides facing and the topstitched edge as the top, pin the small block to the large one with bottom and side edges even as shown in the assembly diagram; baste together along the raw edges. Using a pencil, lightly mark 4 vertical channels, each 3 inches wide, across the small block. Stitch through all layers on each marked line.

See *Binding a Project* for instructions on making and attaching the binding. Bind all edges of the project, folding the raw ends under neatly at the corners to finish.

Make the tie as directed in *Loops & Ties*. Stitch the middle of the tie to the middle of the right side edge of the project.

Index

About the Author

Linda Macho Seward, author of *Patchwork Quilts for Kids You Love* (Sterling, 1985), *Christmas Patchwork Projects* (Sterling, 1986) and *The Complete Book of Patchwork Quilting & Appliqué* (1987), is an active needleworker and designer. She graduated with honors from Tobe-Coburn School for Fashion Careers, and has a B.S. degree in home economics from Douglass College, Rutgers University. Many of her designs have been published in needlework magazines. During her career, she has edited many needlework and crafts books, and now lives in London with her husband and daughter, where she spends a great deal of time at her typewriter and quilting frame.